PAINS in PUBLIC

FOR THE INTOLERANT EVERYWHERE

PAINS IN PUBLIC

50 PEOPLE MOST LIKELY TO DRIVE YOU COMPLETELY NUTS!

ANDREW HOLMES AND DAN WILSON

CAPSTONE
be inspired!

First published 2004 by
Capstone Publishing Limited (a Wiley Company)
The Atrium, Southern Gate
Chichester, West Sussex, PO19 8SQ
www.wileyeurope.com
Email (for orders and customer service enquires): cs-books@wiley.co.uk

ISBN 1-84112-641-1

Designed and typeset by Baseline, Oxford, UK
Printed and bound in Great Britain by TJ International Ltd, Padstow, Cornwall
This book is printed on acid-free paper responsibly manufactured from sustainable forestry
in which at least two trees are planted for each one used for paper production.

Substantial discounts on bulk quantities of Capstone Books are available to corporations, professional associations and other organizations.

For details telephone John Wiley & Sons on (+44) 1243-770441, fax (+44) 1243-770571 or email corporatedevelopment@wiley.co.uk

Contents

Pains – A Catalyst for social change ... 6
Acknowledgements ... 7
THERE'S NO ESCAPE ... 8
THE ARGUERS ... 12
THE ARMCHAIR CRITIC ... 16
THE ATTENTION SEEKER ... 20
THE BRIT ABROAD ... 24
THE CELEB ... 28
THE CHARITY CHUGGER ... 32
THE CHAV ... 36
THE CLIQUE ... 40
THE COLD CALLER ... 44
THE CRAP PARENT ... 48
THE DAWDLER ... 52
THE DINNER PARTY PONCE ... 56
THE DOGGER ... 60
THE DOGMESS MERCHANT ... 64
THE DREADFUL DRIVER ... 68
THE FLESHPOT ... 72
THE GANG ... 76
THE GRAFFITI ARTIST ... 80
THE GULLIBLE GROAT ... 84
THE HOBO ... 88
THE KILLJOY ... 92
THE LADETTE ... 96
THE MOVIE-GOING MORON ... 100
THE NIGHTMARE NEIGHBOUR ... 104
THE NOISY GIT ... 108
THE PARKING POLICE ... 112
THE PARTYGOER ... 116
THE PENSIONER ... 120
THE PLANE PAIN ... 124
THE POLLSTER ... 128
THE PROTESTOR ... 132
THE PUBLIC POLLUTER ... 136
THE PUSHY SALESMAN ... 140
THE QUEUE JUMPER ... 144
THE RAGING BULL ... 148
THE RELIGIOUS NUT ... 152
THE RESTAURANT RAT ... 156
THE SCHOOL RUNNER ... 160
THE SMOKER ... 164
THE SOAP OBSESSED ... 168
THE SPEED CAMERA ... 172
THE STRESSED-OUT SHOPPER ... 176
THE SUPERMARKET SADIST ... 180
THE SURLY SHOP ASSISTANT ... 184
THE SWIMMING POOL PRAT ... 188
THE TARDY TRADESMAN ... 192
THE TOURIST ... 196
THE TOXIC TEENAGER ... 200
THE TRAVELLER ... 204
THE UNEXPECTED VISITOR ... 208
Afterword ... 212

Pains – a catalyst for social change

*W*ho would have believed it? *Pains on Trains* was a bestseller and – of course – a great read. But there's more to this Pain-Spotting business than meets the eye. That book changed the way we commute. No sooner had the Broadsheet been exposed than the quality newspaper publishers started to ditch their broadsheet formats in favour of tabloids. First the *Independent*, then *The Times*. There's only the diehards left – the *Guardian*, the *Financial Times* and the *Telegraph* – but I'm sure it won't be long before they too succumb to the power of Pains. Then Hannah Watts, a student at Chichester University, decided to base her dissertation on *Pains on Trains* and staged a play in a mocked-up tube carriage. All your favourites were there: the Pervert, the Broadsheet, the Sleeper... I have also heard stories of avid Pain Spotters identifying and ticking off the Pains as they journey to and from work. *Pains* is changing the way we think and behave.

Recently we have turned our attention to the office where *Pains in the Office* is already altering the way we perceive our colleagues. Before long we'll either have a new and happier environment in which to work or we'll have open warfare. I think the latter is more likely. Now it's time to look at the public arena and see how we can change the way we behave in the wider world. My prediction is that within the next three to five years the world will be a happier and more considerate place. I also predict that in the not too distant future I will be awarded a gong for public service and social change. See you at Buckingham Palace.

AH

Acknowledgements

Like any book, there are always people who provide invaluable input. I would like to highlight a small number of these observant ladies and gentlemen. They are: James McColl, Sally Hardless, Alistair Kett, Philip Highe, Nick Birks, Rhona Ions, Linda Latham and most of the whole world's population. I would also like to thank Dan Wilson, who has made another fantastic job of injecting some wonderful humour through his images; John Moseley, my editor at Capstone, and of course Sally, who tolerated me writing two books back-to-back without suing for divorce. Sally, you are my rock and I love you with all my heart.

There's no escape

Getting time out from the hustle and bustle of working life is something that we all love to do and certainly need. Many of us carve out a piece of heaven to which we can retreat when we have had enough of this world. So whether it is reading a book, playing sport, going to the cinema, walking in the mountains or getting some retail therapy, we all have something which gives us time for ourselves. Such periods of rest and relaxation are all too short when compared to the time we spend at work and on things that need to be done like paying bills and sorting out domestic problems. That's why, for many of us, retirement is the only thing we look forward to when we go off to work each morning. Unfortunately with few people saving enough for their pensions and companies ripping their employees off through the removal of final salary pension schemes, even this light at the end of the tunnel is slowly being snuffed out.

I believe that when you take people out of the contrived conditions of work, where everyone puts up a façade in order to survive, you should expect to see them as they truly are. And I naively believe that once out of the office people will be polite, treat each other with respect and generally make the world a delightful place in which to exist. Unfortunately, this is far from being the case. In fact my observations suggest that the converse is true. Most people treat each other just as badly outside work as they do inside. Many are complete and utter bastards with no manners. We have rude people, arrogant people, people who want to blow other people up, brawlers, thugs, perverts, crap parents, bad drivers... the list goes on and on and on. The world has become a nasty place full of nasty people. But why?

Part of the problem lies with the world of work, which is becoming more stressful for more of us. Weekends provide little time for rest and relaxation after a long working week. People are just as frazzled on Saturday and Sunday as they are on any given weekday. Another dimension to our predicament is that we are all becoming less tolerant of those around us. In the past we were more likely to cut others some slack, but not any more. We expect instant gratification and if we don't get it we get very annoyed. We don't trust anyone because in the main they cannot be trusted. From lying politicians to corrupt public servants, from self-serving CEOs to unwilling workers, each and every one helps to engender a spirit of suspicion and mistrust that spills over into the public domain. We are also much more focused on ourselves than on the community. No one really cares for the other people around them; cities, towns and villages are becoming soulless shells full of self-centred, hollow people. The final issue is that people's behaviour is also getting much worse. With lives that are less than satisfying many turn to drink, drugs and other substances that provide them with much-needed diversion. So there you have it. All that's wrong with the world in a nutshell. So what can be done? Well, nothing really apart from creating an outlet for the long-suffering everywhere. And here it is, *Pains in Public*.

USING THIS BOOK

This book is all about those people who aggravate you in the public domain. You may have already come across those people that annoy you on your journey into work (see *Pains on Trains*) and at work (see *Pains in the Office*); now it's time to witness how they make your life a misery in every other conceivable environment. Taken together this means that most of your waking hours are spent with people you would rather have exterminated than spend any time alongside. The many thousands of experienced Pain Spotters amongst the readership will know how to use this book but, for those who don't, it is designed in a way that allows you to spot some of the most annoying people you could ever hope to meet, whilst at the same time expressing your own inner feelings in an accessible way. I am writing what you are thinking. Thus, in the same way that bird spotters identify the Lesser Spotted Warbler, this book helps you to spot the Charity Chugger, the Public Polluter and the Ladette. But it goes beyond that, as it identifies how you can avoid them and seek your revenge – if you are brave enough.

Each entry includes:

- The general characteristics of the Pain (including anecdotes and stories).
- Their annoyance rating, which rates the Pain from 1 (limited annoyance) to 10 (extreme annoyance).
- Their rarity, which rates the Pain from 1 (exceptionally rare) to 10 (very common).
- Any seasonal variations, which will identify any changes in the Pain's behaviour.
- A range of avoidance/revenge strategies (with suitable escalation).

At the end of each entry I have also given you, the reader, an opportunity to record that you have spotted the Pain and add your own annoyance rating. Like any "spotting" pastime it has to be interactive, fun and have a sense of purpose to it. You might choose to swap entries with your friends and families as well as with anyone you might meet in the street or down the pub. This volume, when taken together with *Pains on Trains* and *Pains in the Office*, provides you with 150 painful people who make your life less satisfying than it could be. Who needs self-help books, as when armed with the three Pains volumes, you can just avoid the jerks, muppets and morons who make life such a drag? Move over NLP; welcome to PS.

The Arguers

I dislike having arguments. I find them mentally draining and after years of watching those around me argue the toss about all manner of trivial issues I vowed to myself that I would do my best not to get involved. According to eminent psychologists, arguing is good for relationships and can help develop more productive and long-term associations. I'm not sure if I believe this one... The policy of avoidance is lost on most people who feel obliged to conduct their arguments in public places, and these people I call Arguers. Why on earth do they do this? I can only assume that most wash their dirty linen in public because they don't have a washing machine at home. I also think that a lot of people are just too stupid to realise that they are making fools of themselves. The principal Arguers are:

- The **Fishwives**, whose role in life is to argue constantly with those around them, whether that means having a go at their errant husbands for being on the booze all night, or their appallingly behaved offspring who run amok wherever they go. The Fishwife is a 24/7 arguer and can be easily spotted by her bright red, angry-looking face, her clenched fists and her wayward hair.
- The **Lovers**. Love's young dream doesn't always run as smoothly as you'd like. I was staying in a bed and breakfast one summer with my family; not a particularly salubrious place, but it served its purpose. We had settled down for the night and were happily sleeping when we were woken up by a couple having a major tiff. This argument was being conducted on the seaside resort's main thoroughfare and, as it was well lit by the

street lamps, we were able to watch the entire spectacle as it unfurled before our eyes. By all accounts the chap had admitted to cheating on his fiancée. Unfortunately for him, he had done so whilst on holiday. You could see it wasn't going to last; quite rightly she was pretty upset and in a fit of pique had thrown her engagement ring into a bush. So there they were screaming, crying, telling each other how much they loved one another and then screaming and shouting some more.

- The **Divorcees in Waiting**. With divorce rates running as high as they are it is no wonder that we see so many couples at each other's throats. They can be spotted around town, in restaurants and in fact anywhere where they can conduct their pre-divorce preparations in public.

- The **Unhappy Families**. As we'll see with the Crap Parent, who also comes later, there are very few happy families out there. Most are screwed up in one way or another; the Crap Parent sees to that. The Unhappy Family is one that is constantly at war with itself. Some friends were taking a Christmas Eve stroll around the village in which they lived. As they were walking along a footpath, which provided a clear view of the houses which backed onto it, they saw a classic family argument. The father was forcibly ejecting his son from the house shouting "Just bugger off!", Mum was crying uncontrollably and the son was bellowing a stream of obscenities. It's great to be in the bosom of your family, don't you think?

- The **Happy Holidays**. It is well known that people usually fall out during their annual break. It isn't surprising, really, because this is normally the only time they actually get to spend with each other without anything else getting in the way. Wives won't speak to husbands and kids won't speak to parents. In many cases they would have been better off saving their money and spending their holidays at home.

ANNOYANCE RATING

3 – I guess the Arguers are more embarrassing than annoying. As they begin to argue you can see the people around them giving them that look which says "God, how embarrassing. You wouldn't catch me doing that." Others will just stand and stare open-mouthed until the show is over.

RARITY

6 – Arguers are surprisingly common. Our stressful lives, full of expectation followed by bitter disappointment, mean that we all have to hit out and blame someone. Who better than our partners, kids and close family members?

SEASONAL VARIATIONS

Arguments happen all year round and we ought to expect to see public arguments from time to time. You should look forward to more Arguers around Christmas when families are thrown together for the **festive season**. As most families cannot stand the sight of each other you should anticipate lots of fireworks. **Holidays** are another great time to spot the Arguers when, having saved up all year for their annual vacation, all they can do is row and piss each other off.

AVOIDANCE|REVENGE STRATEGIES

1. Avoid having an argument at any cost and never wash your dirty linen in public.

2. Sell tickets for the argument, with a "Roll-up, roll-up, get your ringside seats here".

3. Break into the Arguers' argument and offer help from a low-cost arbitration service.

4. Pose as a security guard, go up to the spectators and say "There's nothing to see here, move along please, move along".

5. Tell them to pull themselves together and get over it.

☐ Tick here when you have spotted the Arguers

RATE THE
ARGUER'S
ANNOYANCE

The Armchair Critic

here is a paradox with knowledge: the more you know, the more you don't know. The best way to illustrate this is to draw a circle. The inside of the circle represents your knowledge (everything you know) about a topic. The outside represents all the knowledge that exists in the world about that topic. The key part of the circle is its circumference, as this depicts how big the boundary is between what you know and what you don't know. A small circle represents someone who knows relatively little. People with small circles of knowledge tend to be ignorant, arrogant know-alls who think they have the answer to everything. They live in a world with limited awareness of how little they know and don't feel motivated to learn anything new. After all, why should they, when they know everything? Welcome to the Armchair Critic. The Armchair Critic is someone with a very limited view of the world who will always have an opinion based upon... well, based upon nothing at all. They live on a diet of trash TV, tabloid newspapers and ignorance. As expected there are plenty of different types, with the two worst offenders being:

- The **Armchair Sportsman**, who is usually fat, has never played any sport since leaving school and yet will be able to tell you how specific sports should be managed. Take football, for example. There are millions of Armchair Footballers who will tell you at great length how the English football team should be dealt with, or how Liverpool's disastrous season is down to their crap coach. They will also say ridiculous things like "We're playing Portsmouth at home tonight", which I find somewhat stupid. First, they don't actually play for the team so how come they use "we" all the time? (I always come back with, "Oh, I didn't know you played for so and so. Where do you play, midfield?".)

Second, they never attend a live match but prefer to watch from the comfort of the settee whilst gulping down yet another can of cheap lager and munching away on burgers, chips and pizzas. And finally, they are boring because all they can talk about is the match last night, or the state of the team.

- The **Armchair Politician**, who will be able to provide critical commentary on the state of the nation's political parties, how the government has got it all wrong and what needs to be put right with the country. These people will have viewpoints on such things as taxation, education, the environment, capital punishment and drugs, and will speak in a serious and committed tone that would convince anyone without a brain. When confronted with any alternative opinion they will become even more animated until they are shouting their views out and spraying their audience with saliva.

Armchair Critics will continue their critical appraisals no matter where they are. Down the pub they will go on and on about the state of the nation whilst slowly getting pissed. When on the road they will appraise your driving ability and provide you with advice on how you should be negotiating the hairpin bend ahead of you. At the dinner table they will quite happily debate any topic so long as their viewpoint is both heard and accepted. The fundamental issue with Armchair Critics is that most of their opinions are baseless and more often than not patently wrong. I was told of a student coming home from his course excited at what he had learnt. Settling down to Sunday lunch with his family, one of his brothers piped up: "The world is round". Now, his father being an arch Armchair Critic interjected "Don't be so stupid, it's a sphere". Our student friend had been studying the shape of the Earth as part of his degree and he stated that it was in fact an oblate spheroid. "No it isn't," said his father. "Dad, it is, I have just been studying it," the student replied. The discussion soon resembled a Punch and Judy show with the father maintaining his line despite being completely wrong. This is typical of Armchair Critics, who believe themselves to be right even when they are ignorant of the facts.

ANNOYANCE RATING

7 –Armchair Critics rate quite highly on the annoyance scale because they are cretins purporting to be geniuses. They annoy because their opinions are based upon what they may have read in the tabloid press or gleaned from all the tripe streamed into their living room via satellite television. None of their ideas or opinions are their own and they are incapable of original thought. What's more, they will never admit they are wrong because they don't even know it.

RARITY

10 – All of us are Armchair Critics of one kind or another and we all have opinions which are insupportable. It's fair to say that the whole population falls into this particular category of pain. However, do look out for the rarer variety which I call the Agent Provocateur. These are the people who will be deliberately controversial in order to stimulate debate and argument. At least they are fun. Well, until people get very angry with them which they often do.

SEASONAL VARIATIONS

You will tend to see much more of the Armchair Critic **before, during and after key sporting or political events.** So watch out for them during things like the World Cup, the Olympics and General Elections. You will also notice the television channels wheeling out all the has-been presenters and critics to provide yet more unsubstantiated facts and bollocks which the Armchair Critics will undoubtedly lap up.

AVOIDANCE|REVENGE STRATEGIES

1. Always back up your opinions with evidence and facts.

2. Ignore the Armchair Critics. If you do this long enough their heads will explode.

3. Send them into the Total Perspective Vortex which they will thankfully not survive once they realise what cretins they are.

4. Suggest they get a slot at Speakers' Corner.

5. Use a combination of superglue and duct tape to seal up their mouths.

☐ Tick here when you have spotted the Armchair Critic

RATE THE **ARMCHAIR CRITIC'S** ANNOYANCE

The Attention Seeker

GENERAL CHARACTERISTICS

ome people are just not satisfied with living a normal life. They want to do something extraordinary and in some way leave a mark on society so that when they have turned to dust they will live on in our memories. It has nothing to do with them doing something useful, you know like inventing the light bulb or the automobile, but rather demonstrates their obsessive desire to capture the public eye and to feel better about themselves. Fortunately, the only mark the Attention Seeker will leave on this planet is a skid mark. A classic Attention Seeker is David Blaine, who spent weeks without food locked in a glass box suspended above the street in Central London. The natural reaction from the population was disdain and cynicism and it wasn't long before people were pelting his box with eggs, having barbecues and fry-ups beneath him and generally making the bloke suffer: the correct response to any Attention Seeker. Even the church is getting in on the attention-seeking act, as only recently did we hear of a priest repeating Blaine's stunt by suspending himself in a glass box above the pulpit – it seems they'll do anything to attract worshippers these days. Such exhibitionist behaviour is not unusual, especially in the United States where you can regularly see nutters doing things to make themselves stand out... for all the wrong reasons. I witnessed some jerk exercising a tortoise in Central Park a year or so ago. There he was, walking at a snail's pace joined to his dawdling pet by a bright red lead, and the only reason he was doing it was to invoke a reaction from all the sad-arsed tourists who probably thought he was wacky and eccentric; indeed, many took photos. The Attention Seeker will get up to all sorts of tricks including walking naked from Land's End to John o'Groats, rolling a pea along the street. They may also cover themselves in silver paint, stand on podiums and remain motionless for hours in the hope that people will throw them some loose change. A knife would be preferable. These street artistes get incredibly upset if their audiences take the piss or photograph them. What do they expect us to do, stand

and clap? Haven't they got jobs to go to? These days we are inundated with Attention Seekers because there are so many avenues for them to exploit, including:

- Reality television, where people who are clearly insane are prepared to be humiliated on the small screen. The Japanese are particular experts at this. The fundamental reason why we have so much reality TV has little to do with giving the great unwashed the opportunity to shine and more to do with cheap programming. Still, when you have millions of people who want to show the world exactly why they are at the bottom of society's barrel, why not?
- Blogging, which is a new phenomenon allowing the average person to describe their mind-numbingly boring lives on the internet, in infinite detail. Worse than doing it is actually logging on and reading such crap. Who cares that someone went shopping yesterday and ate a plate of spaghetti?

- *The Guinness Book of Records*, which gives every Tom, Dick or Harry the opportunity to be forever enshrined in print for farting six thousand times in one minute, eating forty eggs whilst lying naked in a bath of baked beans or pushing fifteen hundred rubber bands up their nose. If you can dream up some ridiculous stunt you can become a member of this very special group of Attention Seekers.

The Attention Seeker also uses more traditional approaches to capturing the nation's imagination including Speakers' Corner, where you can see all manner of nutcases spouting on about God, politics, war and the relative merits of renewable energy. Oh, to set ourselves apart from the proletariat. Politicians and their cronies do much the same. Supporters will pay cash to their favourite political party not because they want to see them succeed, or because they hold deep ideological beliefs, but in order to gain that elusive peerage that will be handed down from generation to generation. At last they think, "I have made something of my life." No sign of cronyism or toadying at all and, from what I can gather, a peerage costs about £100,000 these days. Ultimately all Attention Seekers have one thing in common: they are rampant self-publicists.

ANNOYANCE RATING

6 – Andy Warhol has a lot to answer for. All this "fifteen minutes of fame" tripe has led to seemingly normal people doing stupid things in order to grasp their precious fifteen minutes... like it's going to make any difference to their lives at all. The most annoying aspect of Attention Seekers is that they want to do it in the first place. Anonymity is a far better, and often safer, option.

RARITY

7 –The Attention Seeker is surprisingly common. A significant majority of the population wants to clamber above the anonymous mass, even if this is momentary. In the end, unless they have done something of historical significance, like starting a war, they are wasting their time. Their actions are about as meaningful as a squashed tomato.

SEASONAL VARIATIONS

None. With so many opportunities for Attention Seekers to get in our faces, we should expect to see them all year round.

AVOIDANCE|REVENGE STRATEGIES

1. Live a humble, meaningful life outside of the public eye and away from all who seek out its siren call.

2. Cover yourself with lard, lock yourself in a fridge suspended above a busy motorway junction and tell the world that you are a famous magician.

3. Write an article that describes the psychological makeup of a typical Attention Seeker. Try and link this to such concepts as existentialism, sexual dysfunction and Buddhism to get the credibility it deserves.

4. Set yourself up as a hitman specialising in eliminating attention-seeking idiots.

5. Do everything you can to disrupt their attention-seeking antics.

☐ Tick here when you have spotted the Attention Seeker

RATE THE **ATTENTION SEEKER'S** *ANNOYANCE*

The Brit Abroad

The Brit Abroad belongs to that class of pain that loves to take painful behaviour beyond our shores and I guess for that we ought to be grateful. They have been around for almost a thousand years. Between the eleventh and fifteenth centuries the English became expert at popping over the channel and beating the living daylights out of the French. Those who followed the likes of Henry V to battles like Agincourt were a thuggish bunch, raping and pillaging along the way and once on the battlefield had no mercy for their natural enemy. Then during the empire-building days of the eighteenth and nineteenth centuries the British, as they had then become, busied themselves taking over great swathes of the world that were not rightfully theirs. So has the twenty-first century brought much change? It seems not. Research has shown that our behaviour overseas is still as bad as it ever was. Admittedly we are no longer killing huge numbers of Frenchmen or raping the natural resources of overseas colonies, but we are still as painful and disruptive as ever. In a list of twenty-four nationalities British visitors were ranked as the worst ones to have. The best tourists were the Germans followed closely by the Americans and then the Japanese. At the other end of the spectrum came the Argentines, New Zealanders, Czechs, Finns, Indians, Irish, Israelis and, last and most certainly least, the British. The British were the rudest, meanest, worst behaved, most linguistically incompetent (but, hey, we do have the lingua franca) and most hated by foreigners. The Brit Abroad is characterised by:

- A dislike of local food. The Brit Abroad will travel thousands of miles to a different country and then complain that no one serves fish and chips. When offered the local cuisine they will come out with statements such as "I'm not eating this foreign muck". If

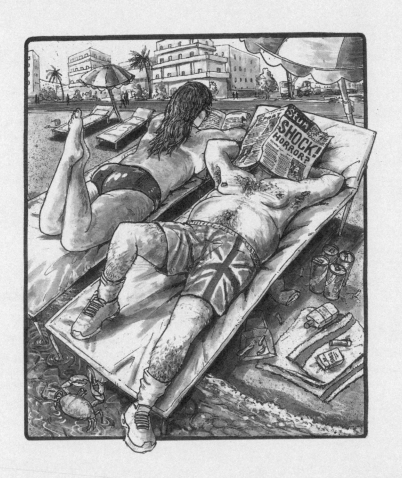

you go to the popular Spanish resorts these days you will be faced with a vast array of British pubs, fast-food outlets and restaurants catering for the narrow-minded Brit Abroad.

- An obsession with boozing it up and getting drunk. Fans of our binge-drinking culture normally get a whole lot worse overseas. Most will spend all morning in bed, all afternoon on the beach topping up their tans, then all evening getting drunk and dancing the night away at some tacky disco. Even the Brits who go skiing fall into the same trap. Authorities in the European ski resorts are so sick of the British getting pissed and causing havoc on the piste that they are now using a combination of breathalysers and speed cameras to catch them in the act. Apparently the British drink more than twice the amount of alcohol than any other nationality.

- Making it sooo obvious that they are Brits by sporting Union Jack T-shirts, shorts and beach towels. They will also sing the theme tune from the *Battle of Britain*, *Land of Hope and Glory* and other well known patriotic songs. The Brit Abroad would be more at home in Henry V's army than on holiday.

- Maintaining their grudges with their historical enemies such as the Germans and French by referring to them as Krauts and Frogs. In one example, a group of Brits rearranged the sun loungers at a hotel poolside into the shape of a Swastika in order to get their own back on the German guests, who always got up early to reserve them.

- A dislike of the locals and of their way of life. The Brit Abroad does not see a foreign country as something that should be appreciated. Instead it is viewed as an extension of Britain and locals are expected to adapt to them, rather than the other way around. People in most tourist resorts hate the summer when they are descended on by hoards of Brits misbehaving, calling them Johnny Foreigners and criticising their ability to speak English. I am sure the irony of this is lost on the Brit Abroad.

ANNOYANCE RATING

6 – If you happen to be a British tourist then I am assuming that, unless you are behaving as badly as they are, you will find their cretinous conduct appalling. I am also assuming that if you happen to be a foreign national from the host country you too will find the Brit Abroad a royal pain in the arse.

RARITY

8 – The increasing ease with which we can now journey around the world has meant that the numbers of these people have increased dramatically. Package tours, charter operators and low cost airlines have facilitated the movement of the Chav (read on) and the great unwashed to the far-flung corners of the Earth. So no matter where you go, you will bump into the Brit Abroad. Good luck.

SEASONAL VARIATIONS

The Brit Abroad can be spotted primarily in the **summer** holidays. Most travel to places like Spain, Greece, Turkey and the Canary Islands where they ply themselves with booze, get sunburnt, eat English food and then come home again. You will spot fewer of them during the **winter** months, unless you go skiing and pick the wrong ski resort, apart from those jetting off to the warmer places of the world. But those who can afford long-haul travel are generally better behaved –

that is, unless they happen to be travelling in business class (see the Plane Pain).

AVOIDANCE|REVENGE STRATEGIES

1. If you wish to travel, behave yourself and appreciate the country which you are visiting.

2. Keep well away from the typical Brit Abroad destinations such as Spain and parts of Greece.

3. Dress up as a local policeman and fine them for inappropriate behaviour. Better still throw them into jail.

4. Make the Brit Abroad a key election issue and get them banned from travelling.

5. Set up a business that teaches the Brit Abroad everything they need to know about behaving atrociously overseas.

☐ Tick here when you have spotted the Brit Abroad

RATE THE
BRIT ABROAD'S
ANNOYANCE

The Celeb

We live in a world obsessed with celebrity and fame. Just cast your eyes over the shelves in any newsagent and you will be spoilt for choice; from B-list stars to philandering footballers, they are all there. Welcome to the Celeb, of which there are a number of types:

- The **Big Time Bigheads**, who are at the peak of their careers. These are the stars and actors who believe that they are above the law; they will always expect to be treated differently. They can beat people up, get drunk on aeroplanes and stop people from looking at them.
- The **B-List Losers**, who are on the way down to oblivion or have never quite dragged themselves up from the gutter of stardom. Such people will do all they can to grab airtime. They will appear on rubbish shows where they have to camp out in the wilderness, eat bat droppings and perform ridiculous trials to win the support of television viewers. They will appear on crass adverts selling anything from sofas to used condoms in the hope to revitalise what little career they have. B-List Losers will always claim to be working incredibly hard on their careers and that this path to stardom started when they were mere babes in arms. One actually stated that he started his glittering career at six weeks old. Hmm, don't think so. More like he had pushy parents who wanted the extra cash and saw a golden opportunity to exploit their new baby.
- The **Desperados**, who are plebeians hell-bent on leaving their nondescript lives to become stars. They will leave their jobs to appear on programmes like *Big Brother* in the hope that this will launch their media careers. Most return to their less than ordinary lives and even for the tiny few that make it, stardom is only a temporary affair. The problem is that they have zero talent.

- The **Ungraceful Oldies** who, having spent the majority of their lives in the media spotlight, can't cope with getting old, infirm, saggy and downright past it. They won't let go. They still strut their stuff on stage when they ought to be wheeling along in a wheelchair. They will spend more on plastic surgery than most people earn in a year and will ditch their long-term partners for twenty-something bimbos or toy boys, and then say that having sex with young people keeps them looking young. Er, no. They are losing their looks, hair and fertility and the only reason why a young filly or stud would want to get near them is because they have loads of cash.

The Celeb will, of course, do anything to grab media attention. They will get drunk, be interviewed about their sexual exploits and orientation, pose for charity, promote chair lifts for grannies, write books (which for those of them who can't write means that someone more literate has to do it for them, assuming this person can interpret their grunts) and claim to have designed lingerie or furniture when, of course, they haven't.

Worse than the Celeb is the Celeb Spotter, who will follow the Celeb in the same way that a puppy follows its owner. Much worse than fawning over celebrities is the desire to emulate their behaviour. For example, cretins will line up to appear on crass television programmes dedicated to pretending to be famous pop stars: "Tonight, Peter, I am going to be Michael Jackson." Perhaps they should say, "Tonight, Peter, I am going to be a jerk." Those obsessed with the lives of celebrities can take things to the extreme. One fan of Jennifer Lopez wanted to look like her so much that he had a sex change and lots of plastic surgery. The 23-year-old man underwent hormone treatment, breast enlargements, buttock implants and face sculpting in order to look the spitting image of Ms Lopez. In twenty years he will look back on this and probably agree it was a tad stupid, especially at job interviews.

ANNOYANCE RATING

9 – I'm afraid that Celebs and Celeb Spotters rate incredibly high on the annoyance scale. The Celebs because they walk around as though they are the most important things in the world, and the Celeb Spotters because they want to live their lives through some star who couldn't care less if they lived or died.

RARITY

7 – With society becoming more fragmented and with fewer people achieving much beyond a pointless existence, many are turning to celebrities and stars to provide them with some kind of meaning. Such people deserve our pity. But they aren't going to get it.

SEASONAL VARIATIONS

None, but Celebs and Celeb Spotters can be seen at key times of the year such as film premieres, awards ceremonies (where a whole bunch of Celebs will turn up and pat themselves on their backs with nauseating, self-congratulatory smiles), pop concerts and book signings.

AVOIDANCE/REVENGE STRATEGIES

1. Never watch television or films, read papers or buy trashy celebrity magazines.

2. Dress up as a famous celebrity and walk round beating people up. When you get arrested claim temporary insanity brought on by your unnatural obsession with the celebrity's life.

3. Set yourself up as a psychoanalyst and offer the Celeb Spotter an opportunity to explore their obsessions.

4. Get selected for the next *Big Brother*, behave outrageously, get the audience to love you and launch your stellar media career presenting children's television... in Albania.

5. Follow Celebs around and hound them in the style of Dennis Pennis.

☐ Tick here when you have spotted the Celeb

RATE THE
CELEB'S
ANNOYANCE

The Charity Chugger

I believe it is very important to do your bit for charity. With so many disadvantaged people in the world, it is both right and proper that the more wealthy amongst us give some of their lolly to the underprivileged. Of course, there are many out there who are tighter than a gnat's chuff and would rather spend their spare cash on another gadget, sports car or kebab. But there are socially minded men and women who believe in helping good causes by walking the streets begging for money – in a legitimate way, you understand. They will shake their collecting tins and buckets, shout out things like "We desperately need your help" or "Please help the blind" and occasionally dress up in fancy clothes, or their uniforms if they happen to be a member of the armed forces or fire service. These are the charity touts. We should respect them for being more generous with their free time than we are. They are relatively inoffensive, but unfortunately they aren't the end of it. The scale of irritation rises with the level of pestering and straightforward charity touts turn into what I call Charity Chuggers. We have to remember that there are many out there who are actually paid to walk the streets, and I'm not necessarily talking about prostitutes. Here we come to the worst subspecies of this pain, the basic, unadorned Chugger – the charity mugger. You can spot them a mile off with their colourful tabards sporting the logo of the latest charity they are supporting. Chuggers are different from the average Charity Chugger because first, they behave like rabid dogs on heat; second, they don't want your cash, they want your bank account details; and, third, they are paid commission. So they really don't give a toss about the charity, they are only in it for the cash. Rarely operating in isolation, you will usually find a whole team of Chuggers snaking their way up the street. Your job is to fight your way through all of them without getting stopped. Often students with nothing better to do they will block your way so that you

either have to engage in conversation or swerve around them. In order to attract your attention they will say such things as "Hi, have you got a minute for one-legged Amazonian dwarfs?" or "What a beautiful smile, ladies, can you spare two minutes for underprivileged tap dancers?". If you are caught they will show you distressing pictures and make you feel bad to the point where you get your pen out and part with your bank details. I recently heard of one Chugger being lectured to by a city gent about how obscene his behaviour was and that he was only doing it for the commission. The student denied all knowledge of payment, even though he had a "salesman of the month" sticker on his tabard. Other over-persistent, though not quite on the same scale, Charity Chuggers include:

- The **Shake Rattle and Roller**, who will shake an almost empty charity box in your face in an aggressive manner as you walk past, like you didn't know they were there.
- The **Enveloper**, who pops a charity pouch through your door every week and then comes back a few days later hoping that you have stuffed it full of more than just buttons and foreign currency.
- The **Charity Sack,** who stuffs an enormous plastic bag through your letter box at least once a month expecting you to fill it up every time. When you do, they never come and collect it.
- The **Rag Weeker**, who as a student has to be wacky, and so will dress up as a nurse, doctor or gorilla (on occasions, all three at once). They run around towns and cities in groups carrying enormous buckets and accosting everyone who gets in their way.

When I was a student I had to contend with the campaigners for Iranian political prisoners who would float around campus. They would come up to you and force a loose-leaf file of graphic images of torture into your face telling you how awful it was and how your cash (what cash, exactly?) could help. When you tried to ignore them or say, "No thanks, bit busy right now", they would chase you down the street, sometimes for a hundred yards. Fortunately, being fit at the time, I could outpace them quite easily.

ANNOYANCE RATING

8 – I always believe that giving to charity is a very personal affair. So when you have some charitable zealot shaking a tin two inches from your face it can be a tad irritating. But it is the full-on Chugger who takes the biscuit here, all positive and hip-hop; they send the annoyance rating right off the top of the scale. Making people feel guilty that they aren't contributing is in the end very unhelpful and turns our generosity gene firmly off.

RARITY

8 – As the population gradually gets taxed to death to pay for the too-numerous-to-mention social change programmes, and as people have turned to gambling (including doing the lottery), drinking and other vices, the amount we give to charity has fallen dramatically. In response the charities have employed an increasing number of people to get into our space in an attempt to get us to part with our folding stuff. It won't be long before there are more Charity Chuggers than people who are willing to give. Perhaps they will just pester themselves.

SEASONAL VARIATIONS

Charity Chuggers, in all their various guises, are with us **all year round**. Come rain, shine, sleet or snow, they will be there, trying to grab your attention and generally making a nuisance of themselves.

AVOIDANCE/REVENGE STRATEGIES

1. Give the Charity Chugger some loose change, and feel good about yourself all day.

2. As you near one look down at your shoes, seem preoccupied and pretend you haven't seen them.

3. Go up to them and say "Charity begins at home".

4. Be sick into the collection bucket.

5. Tell them you've got something in your pocket and as you pull your hand out give them the V-sign and walk off.

☐ Tick here when you have spotted the Charity Chugger

RATE THE
***CHARITY
CHUGGER'S***
ANNOYANCE

The Chav

uring the 1960s Mods and Rockers would descend on the beaches of the south coast and beat the living daylights out of each other with chains. During the 1970s we had the Disco Bums and Punks, with the flares and shiny slacks being kicked into touch by the drainpipes and safety pins. Now we have the Townies and Skaters. Such miscreants belong to the type of pain known as the Chav. The term apparently has its roots in Chatham, which is considered to be the home of the Chav, given that it seems to be overrun with them. The Chav is part of the burgeoning underclass and set themselves apart from the rest of the population by their ignorance, mindless violence, bad taste and delinquency. The Chavs of yesteryear, who were heavily into grunge culture and dropped out of mainstream society, are now one of the most depressed groups in society. Having frittered away their chances to educate themselves they are now firmly on the crap heap, flipping burgers. It might have been cool to hang around street corners in ill-fitting jeans listening to grunge music when you were eighteen, but unfortunately when you are thirty and working in a fast food outlet things don't look quite so cool. According to commentators, modern-day Chavs can be identified by what they wear, which usually incorporates some or all of the following:

- Headwear, which may be a baseball hat pulled over the eyes or a woolly-tea-cosy-like affair that shields the unwashed hair.
- Jewellery, but not the sort you'd buy in a decent shop, more the bling-bling trash sold at the lower end of the high street. You know the sort, thick gold chains, rings with sovereigns embedded in them, enormous gold bangles and huge looped earrings.

- Hooded tops that make them look like hoodlums waiting for their next mugging victim.
- Prison-white trainers which must be pristine, completely without any marks to make them look as though they have just been purchased.

Female Chavs can be spotted by their council house facelift (the effect a tightly pulled bun has on the face), their short skirt that displays mottled legs, the enormous amounts of bling-bling and, of course, the male Chav hanging off their arm. You will normally see hundreds of Chavs at football matches. They turn up in their thousands, wearing the obligatory football shirts which normally hang vertically over their enormous beer guts, bling-bling necklaces and sovereign rings. Another favourite companion is a ferocious dog. The dog, which often has a suitable name like Killer or Fang, tugs on its chain and growls at anything that gets in its way, including the Chav's own children. I was informed of a couple of Chavs who were boarding a train when they asked a fellow passenger where they could put their bikes. The passenger intimated that he didn't know, so with a "F**k this!" they threw their bikes onto the platform and boarded the train without them. It is interesting to see what happens when a Chav strikes it lucky on the lottery, as one did. A former dustman won almost £10 million and yet this newfound wealth made not one jot of difference to his lifestyle. He may live in millionaire's row, but his inability to steer clear of the law has remained as strong as ever. At the time of winning the jackpot, this Chav was wearing an electronic tag for being drunk and disorderly and had been in court thirty times. Soon after his win he was fined for claiming benefits whilst employed. He then spent four months in jail for criminal damage, driving whilst disqualified and taking a vehicle. Not satisfied with this brush with the law, he was then done for possessing cocaine and a clutch of driving offences. Apparently he is down to his last £500,000 having spent most of the money on houses, cars and jewellery. As one police officer remarked, "I wish he'd spent some of the money to move to another country." You can't keep a good Chav down.

ANNOYANCE RATING

7 – For the class-ridden middle classes the Chav represents everything they detest in society – laziness, unruliness, delinquency and no taste. Quite simply, they hate them.

RARITY

9 – It seems that everyone wants to be a Chav these days, from famous celebrities who want to dress like them through to the children's television presenter who desperately wants to be seen as an acceptable member of the underclass, rather than some middle class public schoolboy who has a bizarre fixation with children, wearing pyjamas and talking like a girl.

SEASONAL VARIATIONS

The Chav will be more inclined to dress down during the **summer** months when the sun is hot and the wind is cool. Stripping to the bare essentials, like shorts, bling-bling and the requisite can of lager is important because it allows them to display their tattoos and the full extent of their disgusting bodies.

AVOIDANCE/REVENGE STRATEGIES

1. Study hard, get yourself a good job and rise above the Chavs.

2. Live in the exclusive end of town, where you will see Celebs rather than Chavs.

3. Make a documentary about underclass Britain and Chav kulture.

4. Build a ghetto away from all the nice people and force all the Chavs to live together in close proximity.

5. Get the Chancellor of the Exchequer to introduce a Chav tax, designed to raise excessive amounts of revenue from bling-bling.

☐ Tick here when you have spotted the Chav

RATE THE **CHAV'S** ANNOYANCE

The Clique

f you are anything like me, your mood and attitude to life changes as soon as you're outside the workplace. The best thing about leaving the office is that you have the freedom to mix with whom you please, not with those you need to in order to get on. From Friday afternoon to Monday morning, as well as every weekday evening, your time is yours to do with as you please. That makes a welcome change, doesn't it? No more Bullies, Nitpickers, Village Idiots or Arse Coverers (all of whom we met in *Pains in the Office*). Well... not quite. Although many people spend their time watching the television and getting fat on a diet of soaps, a large proportion will play sport, join clubs of various kinds and mix with other people. After all we are social animals and few of us like to be alone – apart from hermits, that is. Our craving for human companionship is a powerful force that drives us to seek out others with whom we share similar ideals, values and views. The problem is that people can still treat you just as badly outside work as they do inside, especially the Clique. The Clique is a group of people who believe that they are superior to everyone around them. You see them almost anywhere a bunch of people congregate – from the Round Table to the local golf club. These are the people who look down on newcomers and anyone else who doesn't fit their mould (it's too much like work, isn't it?). Sports clubs are particularly prone to cliquish behaviour because of the ability spectrum. Those who consider themselves to be at the top end of the ability range look down on those who are, quite frankly, crap. No one wants to play with the amateurs and no one wants to talk to them either. The Clique will stand there all pucker-lipped, looking aloof and anally retentive; not so much as a "Hi, how are you?" or "Welcome aboard, I'm Peter". The poor newcomer hovers uncomfortably at the edge of the group not knowing what to say or do. I heard of an archery club that was so cliquey that the only way you could get anyone to talk

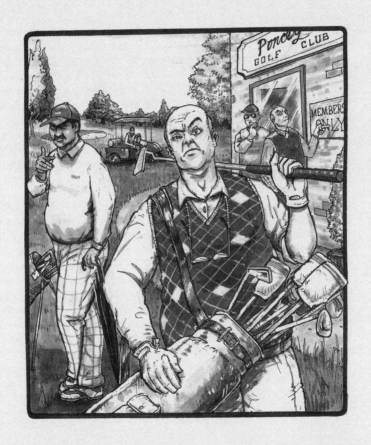

to you was by buying the latest and most expensive bow, but purchasing expensive equipment was a rite of passage that only a few were willing to undergo. In the end the club was left with a small clique of founder members who would pose with their fancy equipment and do everything by the book, and the rest who would turn up to have a bit of fun, laughing, joking and farting on the line. Whatever the setting, the Clique don't allow people to have fun because they take all of the bad things associated with the workplace and revisit them on the club, be it a sports club, social club or whist club. They impose rules and regulations, control everyone around them and jockey for power, especially for the position of chairman or honorary president. If you asked the members of the Clique what they did as their day jobs, you'd find most of them in positions without power or authority, which explains why they want them both outside work.

Golf clubs are notoriously cliquey. They will only admit certain members of society which, as you'd expect, excludes people like the Chav and others who aren't middle class. The only reason they charge such extortionate joining and membership fees is because it keeps all the poor people out. Golf clubs are generally frequented by pot-bellied middle-aged men and retirees wearing sissy tops and Rupert Bear trousers. The clubs are known for their sexism, snobbery, infighting and politically charged committee meetings; not much different from work really. I'm with Oscar Wilde on this one… golf is a good walk spoilt. Every activity and any situation can fall victim to the Clique, take pubs. If you have ever walked into a village pub you'll know what I mean; it's like a spaghetti western in which the hero walks through the saloon bar doors. As they open the music stops, everyone comes to a complete standstill, turns and stares at the newcomer. At this point our hero would walk up to the bar and order a whisky whilst everything returned to normal. In our village pubs, people just continue to stare and you can either order a drink, consume it very quickly and retreat, or just turn on your heel and find somewhere more inviting to seek refreshment.

ANNOYANCE RATING

4 – This all depends on whether you're part of the Clique or not. If you are a member of that sacred inner sanctum, then you will feel just fine. In fact, most of your issues will be with the jerks that remain outside the Clique. However, if you are an outsider who has recently joined the group or someone who is looked down on by the Clique then you will find them very annoying indeed. Quite frankly, if I were you, I'd bugger off and find something more fun to do, like killing them.

RARITY

6 – There are a surprising number of Cliques in the world. You can find them wherever the need for organisational skills is required. I have noticed that retired people love the whole Clique thing; fighting to become mayor, organising the village fete and running the church. Maybe it's because they have nothing else to do or they find it difficult to cope with retirement which, as they say, is a great leveller. So is a bulldozer. Now there's an idea.

SEASONAL VARIATIONS

There are **no seasonal variations** to this pain's behaviour.

AVOIDANCE/REVENGE STRATEGIES

1. Politely introduce yourself to the Clique, begin to build relationships with them and gradually ease yourself into the close-knit group.

2. Only ever take up solitary hobbies and pastimes.

3. Become the anti-clique. Be nice to people, welcome new members, make everything you do together fun – and completely ignore the Clique.

4. Choose a sport which is renowned for being cliquey, pay to be trained to Olympic standard and then turn up out of the blue and wipe the floor with all the supposed experts.

5. When the Clique ignores you, go up to them and shout "What's your f***ing problem?" and give them a Glaswegian Kiss.

☐ Tick here when you have spotted the Clique

RATE THE
CLIQUE'S
ANNOYANCE

The Cold Caller

The Cold Caller is the first of the pains that likes to disturb you whilst at home. There are others, the most notable being the Unexpected Visitor, whom we will encounter later. Cold calling is a technique used by sales and marketing companies to get you to spend money on their products and services. It involves trawling through telephone directories and selecting a bunch of numbers for an operative to ring. They will then call you at the most inopportune moment, which is usually just after you have settled down to your evening meal or the moment you get in after a long stint in the office. Let's face it, the last person you want to speak to is some cretin that you don't even know trying to sell you something you don't even want. What is so annoying about Cold Callers is the way they always start the conversation in that insincere way by asking how you are. Christ, I don't even know the guy and he's prying into my private thoughts already! With the niceties out of the way, it's straight down to the purpose of the call which always entails them attempting to sell you something. They'll also try and get you to buy insurance you don't need and credit you don't want. There are a number of tactics that can be used to deter and frustrate the Cold Caller, including:

- Keeping them on the phone for hours. One guy told me how he will engage Cold Callers for ages, exploring the various products and services they have on offer, the financing options and so on. After a lengthy call, in which the operative on the other end of the line is salivating at the prospect of a big sale, the guy will say "Sorry, changed my mind" and hang up. Be aware, though – extreme patience is needed to employ this tactic.
- Asking for a home telephone number and saying that you will call them later. As it is unlikely that they will be allowed to give you the number this should get them off your back.

- Telling them that you have left some vegetables boiling on the cooker and you'll be back in two ticks. Leave the receiver on the table and settle down to your favourite sitcom. Nine times out of ten, they'll still be on the phone when it finishes. If they are, say "Goodbye" and hang up.
- Inventing excuses that get them off your back. For example, I am regularly rung up by spotty students trying to get me to donate money to their hardship fund. When I was at university, the only students who were hard up were those who spent their cash on new stereos and booze. So why on earth should I give my money to a bunch of undeserving layabouts who can't buckle down and study? My best ploy is to say that I am funding my own kids though college and, because of tuition fees, this is costing me at least twenty grand a year. I have been using this excuse for at least three years and given that my children are several years away from even thinking about university, I reckon it will keep me going until I'm retired. The other one I tried recently, which proved highly successful, was to tell them that Mr Holmes had moved house and had not provided any forwarding address. There was no response from the perplexed student on the other end of the line. Great!

Cold Callers themselves often complain that they are not appreciated and that the people they phone up give them abuse. And so they should. What right has the Cold Caller got to ring you up out of the blue and try and save you five pounds on your annual gas bill? If I was that desperate, I would turn my heating off for a day or two. Cold calling is no longer restricted to the telephone, as we now have to contend with their electronic friends, the Spammers. Spammers are just as annoying as the Cold Callers, although at least you don't have to speak to them. Email inboxes are increasingly clogged up with all manner of spam seeing if you are interested in increasing the girth and length of your penis, watching uncut movies of the sexual exploits of famous people, stealing other people's emails, improving your life with Viagra and so on. Fortunately spammers are now being tracked down in the same way as international terrorists.

ANNOYANCE RATING

8 – Anything that intrudes into our spare time which we haven't initiated is annoying, so on this basis the Cold Caller rates very highly. Why can't they sod off and stop wasting our time? If we really wanted to take out a loan and end up mired in debt, we would become students.

RARITY

8 – Thankfully the number of Cold Callers seems to have reduced over the last couple of years, but that may be because more and more of us are getting our calls blocked by the Telephone Preference Service. In the UK some 4.4 million people have signed up for this service and around 55 million have done so in the US. Irrespective of the help at hand, the Cold Caller and Spammer are still pretty common.

SEASONAL VARIATIONS

There are **none**. The Cold Caller has targets to meet and if that means calling you over the weekend, they will. The Spammer is also with us all year round, clogging up our mailboxes with all manner of emails.

AVOIDANCE/REVENGE STRATEGIES

1. Unplug your phone from the wall so that you can't be disturbed.

2. Leave an answerphone message that states that all Cold Callers should be electrocuted.

3. Engage them in lengthy conversations about how depressed you have become because of all the nuisance telephone calls you've been getting from Cold Callers.

4. Get hold of the home telephone number of the marketing/sales company's CEO and keep ringing them up to sell them some call-blocking software.

5. Scream, shout and verbally abuse them until they hang up.

☐ Tick here when you have spotted the Cold Caller

RATE THE COLD CALLER'S ANNOYANCE

The Crap Parent

There can be no doubt that the fine art of parenting has long since disappeared. Look around you and what do you see? Crap Parents making a crap job of bringing up their crap offspring. Of course there is no manual for bringing up children: well, apart from all the tripe produced by child psychologists. The Crap Parent is someone who couldn't resist the strong urge to procreate but is expert at resisting the need to look after the product of their thirty seconds of ecstasy. The Crap Parent is someone who:

* Will leave their children at home so that they can go down the shops or even away on holiday. One chap was recently in court for leaving his children whilst he went to the shops. Whilst dad was out, one of his kids decided to start a fire so that he could put it out with his toy fire engine, which was clearly unsuccessful given that the house almost burned down and the children had to be rescued.
* Constantly turns to their brats and shouts at them, beats them and generally humiliates them, usually in public. I saw one man turn to his daughter, who was clearly pestering him to buy her something, and shouted "Shut iiiiiiiiiitttt!". The man's face was barely two inches away from his little girl and he sprayed spittle all over her like a water sprinkler.
* Attempts to sell their kids. OK, this may seem extreme, but there have been cases in the United States of parents trying to exchange their children for cigarettes, alcohol and money. One guy stopped people in the street in the hope that he could offload his boy for a bargain basement, one day only, offer of $1,000.
* Pushes their kids so that they can be great successes in life, either that or abject failures, suicide candidates, teenage parents or the smart arse no one likes. They force them to

take up hobbies they can't stick, sit unnecessary exams in order for them to get into the best schools, shove them into university at the age of 11, make them pursue careers they hate and help them lose all sense of being a child. Such parents should get a life. This particular type of Crap Parent is prevalent within the middle classes.

- Lives their life through their children. You hear them in the school playground, in pubs, restaurants and in fact anywhere extolling the virtues of their talented children. They will say such things as "Oh, I have such high expectations for Johnny, he'll be a talented lawyer some day" They will also come out with statements like "My two go to a school for gifted children". Looking at their talentless parents, you do have to wonder where the infant prodigies got it from... the postman, perhaps?

The outcome of all this bad parenting is, as you would expect, future bad parents. The kids brought up by the truly Crap Parent are often foul-mouthed and ill-mannered. A friend of mine went to a wedding recently and approached this beautifully turned-out little girl. There she was, in a lovely pink dress, with perfectly styled hair and pretty little gloves. The man lent over and asked, "What's your name?" Her response was, "F**k off you old c**t!" Charming. To see if you are a Crap Parent, try this simple test by answering yes or no to the following questions:

- Do you immediately jump to your children's defence whenever they are criticised?
- Do you want everyone to think your kids are the greatest that ever lived?
- Do you protect your children from the consequences of their actions?
- Do you justify your kids' behaviour, no matter how bad?

If your answers are mainly yes, then you are indeed a Crap Parent. So are the rest of us. Welcome aboard.

ANNOYANCE RATING

8 – The Crap Parent annoys everyone. Other parents look at them with contempt as their children run amok, thanking God that their clutch are perfect *(yeah, right. Two minutes later, their brats are doing exactly the same thing)*. Pensioners will look on in horror and say such things as "We never had this in my day. Children were to be seen and not heard". Well, either that or shoved up a nearby chimney.

RARITY

8 – The numbers of Crap Parents have grown significantly over the last couple of decades. Astonishingly, some people would rather go to work than bring up children; may I humbly suggest they read *Pains in the Office* in order to realise why this is such a bad idea? However, with the recent and continuing reduction in birth rates, as the young decide to forgo childbirth in order to pursue glittering careers, getting pissed and casual sex, the numbers of Crap Parents will undoubtedly fall.

SEASONAL VARIATIONS

None. Crap Parents are everywhere and you should expect to see them wherever you go. In fact you might be one of them yourself, which means that for you at least, there is no escape.

AVOIDANCE|REVENGE STRATEGIES

1. Never have children. In that way you can just be crap without having to be a parent too.

2. Write a book sharing your experiences as a Crap Parent and, who knows, you might get onto daytime television.

3. Invent a genetic test for Crap Parents, which can be administered early in life, and sterilise those who fail.

4. Film the antics of the Crap Parents and ask if they would like to appear in a reality TV show called *Parents Behaving Badly*.

5. Dress your child up as an angel and parade her through the streets in order to demonstrate just how perfect she is. Why not include a number of testimonials from neighbours, the headmistress and the local priest?

☐ Tick here when you have spotted the Crap Parent

RATE THE
CRAP PARENT'S
ANNOYANCE

The Dawdler

Our lives are becoming more and more frenetic. Life becomes a blur as we hurry from one thing to another whether it is rushing through our workload in the office, speeding through meals because we don't have time to eat at a leisurely pace or ferrying our kids from one party to another. There is barely a moment to relax. The problem is that after a while this becomes the normal state of affairs and slowing down is almost impossible without some kind of psychosomatic response – or death. So it is right and proper that the Dawdler should appear in this volume of the *Pains* trilogy. The Dawdler is someone for whom the word "fast" has no meaning. It is not in their vocabulary and probably never will be. In fact the Dawdler is more like a sloth than a human being. They are particularly slow on their feet, walking at a snail's pace. I hate being stuck behind someone who is walking very slowly, especially when it is too busy to pass. They poddle along oblivious to me behind them, clicking at their heels. As I move from one side to the other to spot an opportunity to overtake, they move into the gap that has just opened up and block my way. You just want to push them aside, which sometimes I do. What I really can't fathom out is how they can walk so incredibly slowly.

The Dawdler is notoriously slow at everything. Even making a decision seems to take forever. I was picking up a dinner suit late one afternoon before trotting off to a ball. I made my way down into the bowels of the shop to find myself at the back of a relatively short queue. My expectations of a five-minute wait were soon thwarted when I recognised that the guy in front of me was a Dawdler. He stood there deliberating with the assistant on which style of jacket to have, how long his trousers should be, what colour bow tie he should choose and so on. He was incapable of making a choice without first entering into

a long debate about the relative benefits of each option. In the end I had to wait for twenty minutes and although from time to time the guy looked over to the other, increasingly impatient customers, his blank expression failed to register any recognition that he was holding up the queue. There must be some kind of neural relationship between the Dawdlers' actions and the amoebas that they seem to have instead of brains. It's no wonder that more of us are getting sick to death of queuing when there are so many idiots in front of us who cannot make a decision. Another favourite of mine is the Bemused. This type of Dawdler is someone who is lost and has no idea where they are. They will stand their ground, mouth open, looking in every direction as they try and work out what to do next. Often found with a map in their hands, they will unfold it and flap it as they work out their bearings. Meanwhile they just can't help but get in the way of everyone else who are attempting to get to their destinations as smoothly as possible. One kind of Dawdler that tends to get up the noses of women is the Stiletto. Unsurprisingly, these are the ladies who wear stilettos, you know the sort, the ones with the six-inch heels. The Stilettos teeter along the street barely able to stand up, let alone walk. Their legs bow outwards as their ankles buckle underneath the weight that is being held up by a three-millimetre square of plastic. Still, who needs sensible shoes when you're out on the pull? It won't be long before the shoes are lying on the bedroom floor, surplus to requirements. There is now an anti-fast movement emerging with authors and Dawdlers alike praising all things slow. As a backlash against the frantic pace with which we lead our lives, the slow movement is attempting to bring us all to a virtual stop. They want slow sex (I guess that must be tantric), slow food (no more burgers and chips), slow driving (well, Pensioners do that already), slow eating (not a bad thing if you want to avoid indigestion) and slow freefall parachuting (hmm, not sure about this one). I can't see how the slow movement will change anything, and I for one don't want to see any more Dawdlers on the street, there are plenty already.

ANNOYANCE RATING

4 – In the great scheme of things the Dawdler is just someone who likes to take their time. Sure they are annoying, but don't forget that it's you getting stressed out, not them. I guess how you feel will also depend on where you live. If you happen to live in a region where everyone is a Dawdler, then you won't get upset at all as you ought to be used to it by now. Go to a city and it will be a capital offence to travel at anything less than ten miles per hour.

RARITY

7 – You will see the Dawdler everywhere, on station platforms, around town, on the street, in shops and in fact anywhere where there are likely to be lots of people. The one factor that is likely to increase the number of Dawdlers is the aging of the population; soon we'll all be shuffling along and getting in everyone's way.

SEASONAL VARIATIONS

None, but the Dawdler is affected by the seasons. During the summer months they slow down because of the intense heat from the sun, whilst in winter they decelerate because they are cold and the weather is bad. During the spring they will be thawing out and during the autumn they'll struggle to wade through all the dying leaves.

You will see the Stiletto most Friday and Saturday nights and you should expect to see the Bemused during the holiday season.

AVOIDANCE|REVENGE STRATEGIES

1. Learn from the Dawdler and understand how being slow might be better for you in the long term.

2. Rewrite the tale the hare and the tortoise, except this time make sure the tortoise gets nuked along the way.

3. Buy some roller blades and get to your destination as fast as possible.

4. Issue them with motorised Zimmer frames.

5. Stick rockets up their arses and light them. Soon the Dawdlers will be travelling at the speed of light.

☐ Tick here when you have spotted the Dawdler

RATE THE **DAWDLER'S** ANNOYANCE

The Dinner Party Ponce

The dinner party is important to the middle-class psyche and is something peculiar to the middle-aged. They create an elaborate ritual around having friends and colleagues round in order to display how middle class they are. The dinner party is a ritual. It starts with the nibbles (crisps, nuts, olives, Bombay Mix if you are feeling particularly adventurous) which no one is allowed to eat until all the guests have arrived, and then only when they are offered around by the host. At an appropriate moment guests are presented with a selection of drinks and invited to talk shite for about half an hour before they are ushered into the dining room to sit down for the meal. Horrible middle-of-the-road muzak will be piped into the room, giving it the ambience of a 1970s supermarket. The small talk, boasting and social positioning takes place over the meal. Ritualistic behaviours aside, the worst bit about dinner parties are the jerks that attend, colloquially known as the Dinner Party Ponces. The typical Dinner Party Ponce is pompous, deeply insecure and incredibly self-centred. Some of the most annoying ponces are:

* The **Name Droppers**, who will go on and on about who they have seen and which events they have been invited to. Such people are terribly boorish with little real conversation apart from such things as "I was invited to a ball at the Italian embassy" or "When I was backstage at the Brit awards, I shook hands with Michael Jackson". Everyone looks interested but feels deeply insecure because they can't come up with similarly fantastic stories.
* The **Hot Topicers**, who will quiz everyone on the latest thing that is in vogue with the middle class. Typical topics for heated debate include the buy-to-let phenomenon, buying second homes in places like Provence, private education and whether or not

women should stay at home to look after the children. They have an opinion on all the major topics of conversation and love to dominate the discussion with their views and ideas on how to change society for the better. Most of the time they are talking complete rubbish and the majority of their observations are invented.

- The **Rude Bastards** love to offend for the sake of it. One story involved a chap who took an instant dislike to one of the guests who had recently moved in with a divorcee whom he and his wife knew. The chap was offensive all night and made the new guy feel very unwelcome. His language was nothing short of appalling and at the end of the evening his wife refused to speak to him.
- The **Stains**, who are the invitees that no one wants to talk to. Once they start they can't stop (a bit like Pringles). They are invited only because they always have been and no one has the guts to tell them where to shove it. One poor chap had the misfortune to attend a dinner party that had a Stain. This Stain, who was known as Big Nose, cornered the guy in the hallway and spent the next two hours talking about his inventions that had been ripped off by other people. What made the whole experience worse was that no one rescued the victim, but why should they? It meant that they were all spared and had a wonderful evening.
- The **Barbecue Boasters**, who like to hold their dinner parties outside so that they can show off their latest state-of-the-art Outback barbecue. They will drone on and on about the quality and workmanship, stating that it was well worth the £1,000 it cost. Like everything middle class, barbecues are as much a status symbol as cars these days. Naturally everyone who attends such events still goes home with salmonella.

Another recent development for the entertaining obsessed is the progressive dinner. This is apparently a new way to make dinner parties more memorable whilst at the same time sharing the preparation. Each course is served at a different neighbour's house so that the party moves from place to place throughout the evening. The event is normally rounded off by everyone meeting at a final location for coffee and liqueurs and perhaps even a quick bit of wife swapping if they want to top the evening off with a bang, so to speak.

ANNOYANCE RATING

7 – Dinner Party Ponces are pretty annoying because they are so incredibly boorish and dull. They believe the party is an excuse to see if they can bore all the other guests to death. Many succeed.

RARITY

8 – Everyone wants to believe they are middle class and hence feels they must display middle-class characteristics. Dinner parties are an essential element of this. So we should expect to see lots of the Dinner Party Ponce. And, with the ranks of the middle classes growing, we should expect to see lots more of them in the future.

SEASONAL VARIATIONS

The middle classes are anxious about their status **all year round**. So they will host and attend dinner parties at every opportunity to ensure they are still perceived as being fully paid-up members of this important socioeconomic group. Most are, of course, nobodies.

AVOIDANCE/REVENGE STRATEGIES

1. Have a take out and get a video. You'll have more fun and won't have to justify your existence to a bunch of status-conscious middle-class twits.

2. Tell the Dinner Party Ponce to shut up and listen to other people instead of talking bollocks.

3. Make up some tall story about how you spent the weekend with the President of the United States and discussed the global economic environment.

4. Accept the first invitation and then, when invited to the next event, refuse on the grounds that it must be your turn to host the party – but never get round to it.

5. Be offensive, tell inappropriate stories and jokes so that you never get invited to a dinner party again.

☐ Tick here when you have spotted the Dinner Party Ponce

RATE THE
DINNER PARTY PONCE'S
ANNOYANCE

The Dogger

If you go down in the woods today you're sure of a big surprise...Parents around the world love singing this to their children, but these days you are likely to be surprised by more than the odd teddy bear tucking into a teacake. Venturing into the woods is not for the faint-hearted, it seems, as there are a number of people who are either having sex or watching other people work themselves up to a climax. Welcome to the Dogger. Dogging originated during the 1970s when the term was applied to dirty old men wondering around woods spying on couples having sex in public. Apparently these blokes would dog the couples' every move in an effort to watch them. And there was me thinking that they were out walking their mutts. According to some, Dogging is an ancient tradition that began with our forebears fooling around on the sand dunes of North Africa. So if you happen to spot an ancient artefact with a pair of pharaohs having a shag on the beach whilst a couple of spear-holding guards looking on, then you know that they are ancient Doggers. Since its modern day revival in the 1970s, Dogging has become a world of its own with exhibitionists and voyeurs satisfying their collective needs in public places, typically car parks, toilets, lay-bys and woods (car parks in particular appear to be a favourite). It wasn't long before Doggers realised that the exhibitionists wanted them to get involved, which avoided the use of the packet of tissues they would carry around with them whilst in the woods. The Dogger can be found in the following forms:

- The **Car Park Perverts**, who will drive into secluded car parks, wait for broad-minded couples to turn up and on the cue of flashing interior lights will don their night vision goggles and watch with foaming mouths as they perform. If they are really lucky, the Car Park Perverts may be invited to join in.

- The **Lay-by Lovers**, who will have sex in lay-bys with anyone that fancies a bit on the side, so to speak. They are perhaps less discerning than the Car Park Perverts because they will try it on with anyone: flower vendors, kebab men, lorry drivers and the odd breakdown mechanic.
- The **Wooded Watchers**, who will give the impression they are innocently walking in the woods when in fact they are out looking for people having sex. They will be armed with binoculars, telephoto lenses and a large tub of Vaseline, all telltale signs that they have more on their minds than the odd blue tit.
- The **Toilet Technicians**, who will meet other people for sex in confined spaces. Perhaps if they like it that much they could get together with the Car Park Perverts and have sex in the boot of a car.
- The **Curious Celebrities**, who will claim to have become interested in Dogging whilst surfing the net and tried it out a couple of times to satisfy their curiosity. We are never quite sure whether they are actually doing it for attention in order to provide some lift to an otherwise flagging career. Let's face it – loads of celebrities like to get caught because it adds to their mystery and provides much-needed media coverage.

Dogging is now going electronic. With the advent of Bluetooth technology, which for those technophobes amongst us allows people with the same technology to send contact details, messages and pictures over their mobile phones, men and women are now getting into "Toothing". Toothing involves hooking up for illicit sex in public places, such as on the train, at conferences and by the frozen peas in the supermarket. One guy was "bluejacked" by a young woman on a train and, after a few exchanges, decided to have sex in a station toilet. Apparently, the whole affair was over very quickly with little in the way of romance. It won't be long before Doggers will be using their mobile phones to watch other people having sex from the comfort of their own homes rather than wading through dog shit and litter in a car park.

ANNOYANCE RATING
6 – This will depend almost exclusively on whether you wish to partake in Dogging activities. If you fancy your chances and you find it exciting, then I guess there is little chance you will find your fellow Doggers annoying. However, you may regret your decision. Also, if you happen to be out walking one evening and bump into a bunch of Doggers (I wonder what the collective term is?) you are likely to be both shocked and upset at their acrobatics.

RARITY
4 – Despite the plethora of websites and chatrooms dedicated to the art of Dogging, the numbers of people involved with such outdoor antics is pretty small. I am sure that this entry will raise some interest so I wouldn't be at all surprised if the popularity of Dogging increases as a consequence.

SEASONAL VARIATIONS
You are more likely to see an increase in Car Park Perverts during the **winter months** when the average Dogger would struggle to perform outside. Watch out for steamed-up windows with feet and buttock cheeks pressed up against them. The **summer** will find both a general increase in the number of Doggers and a larger number of Wooded Watchers, Toilet Technicians and, if you're really lucky, the odd Curious Celebrity.

AVOIDANCE|REVENGE STRATEGIES
1. Never stray into car parks at dusk, toilets at night or woods on a sunny afternoon.

2. Always be wary of people sitting in their cars with flashing interior lights.

3. Dress up as a car park attendant and issue the Doggers with fines for illegal parking.

4. Buy a double-decker bus and drive around the country offering group Dogging sessions to desperate motorists.

5. Film a number of Dogging sessions and send them into *TV's Naughtiest Moments*.

☐ Tick here when you have spotted the Dogger

RATE THE
DOGGER'S
ANNOYANCE

The Dogmess Merchant

A lot of people have pets. Some of these are quite strange, such as snakes or tarantulas, whilst others are less so, such as hamsters or guinea pigs. As a child I had all manner of pets, in fact our home was more like a menagerie at times, so I can understand the fun that pets can provide. Then there are dogs and, more importantly, dog owners. I never saw the fascination of dogs and still don't. They stink your house out; they are worse than having children because, unlike kids, they never grow up; the owners are usually covered in dog hairs and – worst of all – they tend to perform their bodily functions in public. How many times have you or I stepped in, or slipped on, the mess left behind by the inconsiderate dog owner and their dog? It's worst when you have stepped in some canine crap and only noticed when you're back in your car or home. By then it's too late; it has become ingrained into the car's carpet or your oatmeal shag pile, or both. Cursing the jerks that let their dogs poo everywhere is a national pastime, particularly when we consider that several tons of dog dirt is deposited on our pavements every day. The Dogmess Merchants, as I like to call them, come in a number of types, including:

- The **Pavement Pooers,** who will walk along the pavement, their dog trailing behind them (usually on a very long lead) sniffing at every lamppost and bush in an attempt to find the best place to lay a fresh turd. Once found, the dog will collapse its rear legs and shake as it forces its breakfast out of its quivering sphincter. The owner is, naturally, looking away and pretending to be oblivious to the goings-on. With a swift tug of the lead, the dog is led away leaving a pile of excrement for some poor sod to tread in.
- The **Crafty Crappers**, who will walk past your front garden and allow their dog to let loose all over your freshly mown lawn.

- The **Playing-Field Planters**, who will release a dog onto a school playing field or recreation ground and let them foul where ever they like. Pity the poor kids doing sport the next morning; a swift tackle or fall and they'll be getting more than a mouthful of turf.
- The **Indiscriminate Idiots,** who have no concerns at all about where their dog decides to defecate, so long as it's not in their back yard.
- The **Seaside Spoilers**, who will walk their dogs on the lovely unspoilt beaches of the world and ensure they mix shite with shells.
- The **Frenzied Fertilizers**, who not content with owning just one dog, love to walk round with a whole pack of them. You can always find out where they live by the trail of dog dirt from their incontinent mutts.

What is so goddamn annoying about the Dogmess Merchants is the supercilious look they have whilst their dogs are dumping in a public space. It's as though it is their right to foul up their local pavements and playing fields. Since when, exactly? Maybe there is some long-lost common law? To be fair there are people who clean up after their canine companions and for that we should be grateful. In fact it is quite amusing watching them scoop down to pick up a freshly laid turd in a plastic bag and then pop it into a pocket. I imagine that this can be very useful in winter, as it provides some additional warmth. The problem with this community-spirited action is that it leaves skid marks and stains all over the pavement that people can still step in. Furthermore, many councils have introduced dog toilets where owners can literally hold their clag-ridden pests over a bin and let them crap into it. (OK, I know it's for the plastic bags, but wouldn't that be more entertaining? Especially if the dog involved was a St. Bernard.) The problem then is getting some poor sod to empty the bin, which I am sure is a vomit-inducing experience. Judging from the stench from these receptacles, particularly in the summer, I reckon they are never emptied. The worst example of Dogmess Merchant behaviour involved a poor old man who was killed by a Dogmess Merchant after complaining that the DM's dog kept empting its bowels onto his front step. So, not content with letting his dog foul someone else's step, the Dogmess Merchant was the one who took offence – bizarre.

ANNOYANCE RATING

10 – The Dogmess Merchant is, I think one of the biggest pains you will meet in public. The way they leave the product of their dog's bottom on the pavement, on footpaths and even in your garden is nothing short of irresponsible. I wouldn't mind if they let their dogs crap on their carpets at home. Mind you, judging from how some dog owners smell, I think this must be true in many cases...

RARITY

9 – With so many lonely and single people in the world, the number of Dogmess Merchants is significant. You see, some people can only find companionship in a dog because they lack the social skills to talk to people. There are some countries in the world that either eat dogs or just don't find them acceptable. Perhaps they could eat the owners too?

SEASONAL VARIATIONS

You will actually see many more Dogmess Merchants in the **summer** months when they feel more inclined to let their mutts run free to crap anywhere they like. But dog mess is with us all year round.

AVOIDANCE/REVENGE STRATEGIES

1. Wear plastic covers over your shoes as a precaution.

2. Prosecute the Dogmess Merchant under the Litter (Animal Dropping) Order of 1991.

3. Scoop up the offending lump and throw it at them.

4. Pose as an environmental health officer and inform them that the penalty for letting your dog drop its guts in public is to have its bottom sewn up.

5. Go to the their front garden, drop your trousers and lay one of your gifts on their lawn. See how they like it.

☐ Tick here when you have spotted the Dogmess Merchant

RATE THE
DOGMESS
MERCHANT'S
ANNOYANCE

The Dreadful Driver

GENERAL CHARACTERISTICS

They always tell you at the end of your driving lessons that you only start to learn to drive after you have passed your test. Although we would all claim to be great divers, I'm afraid that there are just too many of us out there who are, quite frankly, crap. Such people I call the Dreadful Drivers. As expected, there are many different types, including – but not limited to – the following:

- The **Vicious White Van Man** who is usually male, works in a trade and often has an IQ of less than 10. These people are universally hated for overtaking in the most dangerous of places and at the most unnecessary of times, like at traffic lights or pedestrian crossings. They will scream past you in first gear, cut you up and then proffer the prongs or single-fingered farewell – like it's your fault.
- The **Mad Motorbiker,** who believes it is absolutely compulsory to overtake any four-wheeled vehicle just because it's possible. Mad Motorbikers will sit on your tail and squeeze into the smallest gap and zoom in between queues on the motorway as though nothing was there. Of course they forget that if they are involved in a road traffic accident they will end up as strawberry jam smeared across the tarmac.
- The **Crazy Cyclist** hates all other traffic and is even worse than the typical motorcyclist. They can be seen wearing their fluorescent clothes and those rather fancy (but quite useless) safety hats weaving in and out of traffic, jumping red lights and mowing down pedestrians especially when they insist on riding at breakneck speed on the pavement. One cyclist hated motorists so much that he slashed the tyres of hundreds of cars causing damage worth thousands of pounds. He believed they were not giving him the respect he deserved.

- The **Boy Racer** who, having just passed the driving test and managed to scrape together a couple of hundred pounds for a clapped-out Escort or Peugeot, will enhance it with wide wheels, a spoiler, loud exhaust and a stereo system with a subwoofer the size of a dustbin. Then, having made these fine tweaks to its appearance, the Boy Racer will drive around town all day and night at ridiculous speed. They love to rev up at traffic lights and intimidate grandmas driving their Morris Minors.
- The **Sunday Afternooner**, who insists on clogging up the roads by driving at ten miles per hour. Sunday Afternooners are usually of pensionable age with failing eyesight and often wear a thick coat and hat, even in a sweltering hot summer. They can barely see thirty inches in front of them, let alone thirty yards. They often see mysterious accidents in their rear view mirror, drive the wrong way down dual carriageways and hate driving in the dark.
- The **Posh Poser.** These people feel compelled to waste their bonus on the latest top of the range sports car in order to demonstrate their wealth, keep up with the Joneses or prop up their flagging sex life; cars are, for many men, a penis extension. I wonder what they are for women.
- The **Fog-Light Fiend,** who insists on putting fog lights on whenever it isn't foggy. They especially love turning them on when it is drizzling, thereby rending the motorists behind them temporarily blind. Such people think they are being community spirited when in fact they are being total morons.
- The **Joy Rider** who, being no more than thirteen and therefore not legally allowed to drive, will steal any reasonably high performance car, drive it around a sink estate and once finished with it, torch it.

Don't think you are any better off overseas. In the US you are more likely to get cut down by the Drive-By Shooter and apparently in the Middle East some people drive like maniacs because as far as they are concerned their lives are in Allah's hands. According to the World Health Organisation, car-related deaths will soon be the biggest global killer.

ANNOYANCE RATING

7 – As pains go, Dreadful Drivers rate highly on the annoyance scale because they are oblivious to all other road users and because of the frustration and annoyance they cause. They are locked away in their little metal boxes protected from those around them. Shame.

RARITY

10 – The Dreadful Driver is arguably the most common of the public-based pains, mainly because there are just so many of them and no matter where you go you will bump into at least one of them, often literally.

SEASONAL VARIATIONS

All year round. You will spot plenty of Dreadful Drivers whenever there is rain, fog or snow, when their ability to drive normally is further impaired and they can't help but crash into the person in front. The summer will bring particular varieties out, such as the Sunday Afternooner, Crazy Cyclist and Boy Racer. Interestingly, there is also a regional variation to the Dreadful Driver. The further west you go the more you will see of the Sunday Afternooner given the preponderance of pensioners, whilst the further north you go the more Joy Riders and Boy Racers you will spot.

AVOIDANCE|REVENGE STRATEGIES

1. Emigrate to a country that doesn't have many cars or roads.

2. Become a Dreadful Driver yourself and see what havoc you are capable of causing.

3. Dress up as a policeman, force them to pay on-the-spot fines and lecture them on the merits of defensive driving.

4. Buy a tank and drive over them.

5. Go on an advanced driving course so that you can pose by performing handbrake turns at ninety miles per hour.

☐ Tick here when you have spotted the Dreadful Driver

RATE THE
**DREADFUL
DRIVER'S**
ANNOYANCE

The Fleshpot

The Human Race is as varied in its shape and size as any other species, and looking at the naked form is something that the majority of us find pleasing. After all, if we didn't there wouldn't be much procreation or a mulit million porn industry, although we may find the human form beautiful, there are plenty of instances of it having the opposite effect. Take rotting corpses, for example. Not much to bring a smile to your face there, unless you happen to be a mortuary assistant. Similarly, the clinically obese don't do much in the genital department. No matter how gross people look fully clothed, the worst thing they can possibly do is to strip off. Those who do are known as the Fleshpots. For some reason Fleshpots love to put various parts of their anatomy on display. From bellies to butts and from todgers to tits, Fleshpots will show them all. For some peculiar reason, the Fleshpots actually believe they are attractive and that it is perfectly normal to leave their belly hanging out over their trousers complete with fluff protruding from their navel. Some of those who prefer to remain covered up seem to accentuate their bodily form by wearing skin-tight leggings or shirts that barely cover their wobbly guts. Such choice of clothes leaves very little to the imagination, but it is still preferable to seeing them semi-naked. The state of undress of the Fleshpot can be viewed along a spectrum which ranges from the fairly innocuous to the downright offensive:

- The **Bouncing Belly**, who insists on displaying a midriff or entire gut despite it being unpleasant to look at. With fashion favouring cut-off tops and hipster jeans, you are often privy to a few inches of flesh which looks quite reasonable on the flat-stomached. Unfortunately rolls and rolls of fat hanging over a waistband is a tad off-putting. A man's beer gut is a case in point. The huge gut on a beer-swilling man is bad enough

when covered by an ill-fitting football shirt, but when they insist on walking round dressed only in shorts it is grotesque. The gut protrudes like a giant peach and glistens as the sun is reflected from the sweat running down it, onto the shorts.

- The **Crackman** can't help but show a butt crack as he bends down. The Classic Crackman is, of course, the builder who insists on wearing baggy jeans which barely cover his arse. When the Crackman leans over you could park your bike between his butt cheeks.
- The **Thong Thing** who, although grossly overweight, wants to walk around in a thong that is barely visible beneath the mounds of flab. Their cheeks will subsume the cheesewire-like thread so it looks as though they are actually naked.
- The **Nudist**, who takes the Fleshpot thing just a little too far by stripping off completely and becoming at one with nature. I always wonder why people want to show off their naked form to people around them; I can only assume that they are exhibitionists. The problem is that most nudists are hardly ideal examples of the beauty of the human form. They walk around with everything hanging out saying how wonderful it is to have the wind rushing though their groins.
- The **Swingers** who, as we all know, love to display their flesh for one reason only – to have sex with as many people as possible. Once again, have you noticed how most Swingers are pig ugly, fat and slightly deranged? I guess when you're stoking the fire you don't look at the mantelpiece. Watching shows that portray the life of a Swinger, especially when on holiday at places such as Hedonism, is an amusing and at the same time vomit-inducing experience.

ANNOYANCE RATING

6 – In the main, the Fleshpot is only mildly annoying. The momentary gawp as they walk past is soon followed by "Did you see that?" and, frequently, laughter. We shouldn't be annoyed with the Fleshpots because they are beacons for us all. If they didn't display their ugly bodies we wouldn't take dieting and keep fit so seriously.

RARITY

6 – If we take any of the Fleshpots individually, we could argue that they are pretty rare. Let's face it, unless we happen to be one, we see very few Nudists or Swingers. But if we include the Thong Things, Crackmen and Bouncing Bellies they become more common. As fashion changes we may see less of some types, but I fear the number of Fleshpots will undoubtedly increase.

SEASONAL VARIATIONS

Although fashion and perversion will dictate how much flesh you will see at any given time, it is the **summer** when you will see more of the Fleshpot. The sun does strange things to people, not least making them lose their inhibitions about stripping off and showing the world their private parts.

AVOIDANCE|REVENGE STRATEGIES

1. If your body is not perfectly formed, keep it covered up. That goes for most of us, then.

2. Offer free belts and cummerbunds to the Fleshpots so they can cover up their folds of flesh.

3. Use an acetylene torch and see if the Fleshpot melts.

4. Create a mural of the various kinds of Fleshpot and title it *The Grotesque Forms of Humankind*.

5. Pose as a plastic surgeon and offer cosmetic surgery to reshape their bodies into something which is more visually acceptable, like a banana.

☐ Tick here when you have spotted the Fleshpot

RATE THE **FLESHPOT'S** ANNOYANCE

The Gang

When I was at junior school, there was a certain amount of kudos in being the leader of a gang. Mine included five other boys and we would terrorise the girls, especially during the summer when we would kick down their grass houses. My friends and I soon grew out of this early gang phase of our lives when we went to secondary school. During my adolescent years I was still part of a large gang who used to drive around the countryside, trash the odd bar and generally have a lot of fun. Being part of a gang gave me and my mates a sense of identity and camaraderie. Now, as I sit at my desk writing, I am no longer a member of a gang and in fact I now find them rather annoying... that's aging for you. The Gang is alive and well and still remains a public nuisance. The Gang comes in all sorts of shapes and sizes, from the Adolescent Gang who will bum around the town during the day looking out of place and spotty to the Hobo Gang who will sit in a large group in an open space drinking cider and swearing at passers-by.

One of the worst variants is the Football Gang. The Football Gang can be spotted from a quarter of a mile away. They will be wearing their team colours and travelling in large numbers looking slightly, if not completely, Neanderthal as their ape-like gait forces them to sway from side to side as they walk. The dead giveaway, though, is the large number of police officers who accompany them on their journey. The Gang's objective is not to watch the sport but to beat the shit out of the other team's supporters. Before we condemn the football hooligan to the back streets of the inner cities, we should accept that they come from all walks of life. Only recently a gang of seventeen hooligans was sent to prison after being tracked down after years of violence. The gang was led by a teacher who controlled

battles between rival gangs using the internet and mobile phones (clearly an expert in new technology and a great advertisement for the teaching profession). What was most surprising about this gang was that most were in their thirties and forties and family men; clearly they had never quite grown out of the need to be part of a gang and cause trouble. A film called Football Factory has been released which glorifies soccer thugs. As expected it has caused a bit of a storm. The film, which portrays the lives of a bunch of Chelsea hooligans, has been hailed as fantastic by a former gang member. When interviewed he said "I can't believe all the fuss it's caused … it's the reality… It's a few people punching each other, it isn't a big deal. It's about camaraderie and respect, about people having a laugh." Really? I must get involved sometime.

The other type of gang that is equally disturbing is the Steamer. A Steamer Gang is a group of youths who will surround their victims on trains and buses as well as in the street. They will knock them about a bit, steal their belongings and then scarper before the victim can identify any of them. Fortunately, like the Football Gang, they are eventually caught and spend time in jail bending down in the shower to pick up the soap. Other gangs include the Hells Angels, Ku Klux Klan, scouts, school children, and pensioners on coach trips. Gangs share a number of characteristics, including:

• Having little or no regard for other members of society.
• Normally being weak individuals who can't stand on their own two feet.
• Looking to a leader to provide them with direction and orders, which they follow blindly. With behaviour like that they really ought to be in the army.
• Loitering, hanging around and generally littering the street with their physical presence.
• Roaming around towns and cities drunk and causing trouble.

In the end I suppose people need to feel a part of something that is bigger and more significant than just themselves. Being a member of a gang gives them that sense of belonging and identity.

ANNOYANCE RATING

7 – Gangs are undoubtedly intimidating to those travelling alone. You can see people avoiding them as much as they can, preferring to walk on the other side of the street.

RARITY

3 – This will depend on where you live. If you happen to live in a village the only sort of gang you will see is the one that comprises all the village idiots who will hang around on street corners and recreation grounds. If you're particularly unlucky, they will stand in your front garden. If you are in a major town, you will see the full range of gangs, from muggers and youths to the Football Gang. In cities you are also more likely to witness gang warfare between rival gun runners and drug dealers. I don't think you can fault city life, can you? It's so colourful.

SEASONAL VARIATIONS

None. The variations in the Gang's behaviour will be driven almost entirely by the nature of the gang itself. So you will see the Football Gang most Saturday afternoons when the matches are on. Although there is unlikely to be much violence before the match, you should expect to see plenty afterward. Steamers will tend to come out during the late evening when they can prey on half-cut office workers and partygoers as they stumble home. And the adolescent gang will mainly be seen at the weekend getting tanked up on lager and generally making a nuisance of themselves.

AVOIDANCE|REVENGE STRATEGIES

1. Avoid any obvious haunts of the gang such as football grounds, deserted wasteland, late or early morning tubes or buses, street corners and your front garden.

2. Walk round in a suit of armour and carry a claymore for defence.

3. Hire a personal bodyguard. With any luck you will be mobbed by beautiful people who think you're a film star.

4. Seek a change in legislation that restricts gangs to two members.

5. Start your own gang, design a fancy uniform and walk round looking cool and menacing at the same time.

☐ Tick here when you have spotted the Gang

RATE THE
GANG'S
ANNOYANCE

The Graffiti Artist

GENERAL CHARACTERISTICS

It is everywhere, from the sides of trains to the walls of buildings. Graffiti, that eyesore that confronts us wherever we go. The graffiti we see today, courtesy of the many Graffiti Artists, started out in New York in the 1970s when it became synonymous with Hip Hop. As Hip Hop grew in popularity a number of people started to create images that expressed its culture and, not satisfied with using posters, decided it would be much more fun to draw over subway walls. Then came Taggers. These were Graffiti Artists who would just write the same thing wherever they went, the first of which was Taki 183. Just when the kids were losing interest in writing incomprehensible bollocks all over walls, trains and any other space they could find, some jerk decided it would be a great idea to run a documentary on graffiti. The result of this fantastic idea was an explosion of graffiti worldwide. It wasn't long before Graffiti Artists were competing and soon rival gangs were covering entire subway trains with their "art". You don't tend to see many landscapes or contemporary pictures, most of the stuff the artists write are tags, which are ugly to look at. Apparently the people that undertake such acts of vandalism are treated like heroes by their mates. I guess that's because they can string more than two letters together to form an elementary word, something their friends have yet to achieve even though they are at high school. The Artists originally used a few coloured pens, a bit like when they were in the infants, but it soon dawned on them that spray paint was more effective. The modern Graffiti Artist will use other devices. For example one, whose signature is BOOM, defaced a number of shops on Richmond Hill in London using a spark plug. Repairs cost £300 per shop. The Tag also appeared on fences and signs along the road as well as on the wall of a restaurant. When caught, which they often are in the US, Graffiti Artists will claim to be merely expressing themselves. But surely, if all they can muster is some three letter

signature, they clearly can't express themselves that well. Judges have a different view which involves them being sent down and a couple of guys were sent to jail for 60 days for spray-painting empty buildings in Detroit. Meanwhile police in Tayside are using digital cameras to take pictures of the offending graffiti in order to ramp up the charges against the artists. And in San Diego they have set up Taggertrap, a six man graffiti task force. So watch out all you Graffiti Artists out there, they're coming to get you.

I have a confession to make here. My mates and I were, albeit briefly, Graffiti Artists. Out Tag was Pantz Sniff 84, which we thought highly amusing. I remember us using it to great effect on a field trip where we caked the walls of our hostel from top to bottom in our newly formed tag. After admiring our handiwork we decided we had better get rid of it before the tutor came into our room. So, in a fit of panic and using a combination of Brut deodorant and vodka, we managed to remove most of it although the paint from the walls tended to come off along with the graffiti (having witnessed the powerful cleaning abilities of Brut I never used it again). Today it seems that graffiti is going mainstream. Businesses are using graffiti as a quick and easy way to relate to a cutting-edge market. Whether it is on T-shirts or in viral marketing campaigns they are turning to graffiti to get their trendy messages across. Maybe this is the end of the Graffiti Artist; if they are anything like the other underground movements they should lay down their spray cans right now. As with so many other things in life, the internet has changed everything. You can now graffiti the web. Yes, you read it right, you can now deface anyone's website with graffiti. All you need is the URL of the website you intend to deface and some fancy graffiti to add to it. So all you budding web vandals out there – get going.

ANNOYANCE RATING

7 - I know that local councils find the Graffiti Artists very annoying indeed, as do most taxpayers. A vast amount of taxpayers' money is spent every year on trying to remove the crap they leave on walls, trains and garages. An average city will spend in excess of £1 million every year and the global cleanup costs run into billions. I wouldn't mind so much, but most graffiti looks so bloody awful. Perhaps if they could paint copies of Constable's *Haywain* people wouldn't care. The other thing that really annoys people is that the bloody stuff is everywhere. No matter where you go you will see it daubed over walls, sidings, windows... god knows what the Graffiti Artist's bedroom is like.

RARITY

9 – I am rarely out at night on the lookout for the Graffiti Artist, so I can't say I've seen that many. But judging from the amount of graffiti I see I can only assume that there are lots of them.

SEASONAL VARIATIONS

Graffiti Artists are a bit like rabbits – **nocturnal** pains that inevitably end up beneath the wheels of a car. I also assume that you should be able to spot more of them during the **summer** months when the rain is less likely to spoil their artwork. As one of the few nocturnal pains, though, it is unlikely that you will ever spot them unless you happen to be an insomniac.

AVOIDANCE/REVENGE STRATEGIES

1. Be wary of anyone who is walking around with cans of paint, especially at night.

2. Find out where the Graffiti Artists live and throw paint all over the walls of their house, windows, front door and car. See how they like it.

3. Catch the Graffiti Artists and spray your own Tag on them, using sulphuric acid.

4. Arm yourself with a powerful anti-graffiti cleaner and model yourself on a famous superhero protecting the middle classes against the sink estate Graffiti Artist.

5. Develop your own tag, like Twat' 21, Arse' 62 or Inhuman Discharge' 96.

☐ Tick here when you have spotted the Graffiti Artist

RATE THE
GARFFITI ARTIST'S
ANNOYANCE

The Gullible Groat

I believe that there are some incredibly stupid people in this world who will believe anything that anyone tells them. Maybe they are naive, maybe they are just too trusting, but in the main I feel they are just intellectually challenged. Such people, who believe everything they are told, are what I call the Gullible Groats. One of the classic examples of how stupid people are was Orson Wells' 1938 radio broadcast of *The War of the Worlds* in which a bunch of Martians landed on earth to wipe out the human race. The Americans who listened to this show were genuinely terrified and actually believed they were being invaded. Even in these media-rich days there still seems to be a huge swathe of gullible people. The Gullible Groat will fall for all manner of hoaxes, scams, frauds and get-rich-quick schemes. They will fall for the pyramid-selling scam, in which they are persuaded to part with their cash to buy products such as household cleaners, water softeners, alarm systems and the like and then try to recruit other people to do the same. The only people who purchase the products are their friends and families who feel pressurised into buying the overpriced crap. Those peddling such schemes will bamboozle the Gullible Groat with prospectuses telling of incredible wealth showing cheesy couples with palatial mansions, fleets of sports cars and yachts on the Med. The reality is more likely to be one in which the Gullible Groat's garage is piled high with the crap they can't sell, they have made barely ten quid in the process and have alienated their friends and family who are sick to death of them trying to offload overpriced shite. The only people who make the big bucks are those at the top of the pyramid. Another classic is the Nigerian investment scam (known as the 419 scam after the section of the country's penal code that legislates against them); in 2003, 150 Britons fell for this and lost £8.5 million between them. One fraudster managed to dupe a Brazilian bank manager out of $242 million – the biggest 419 scam ever. The

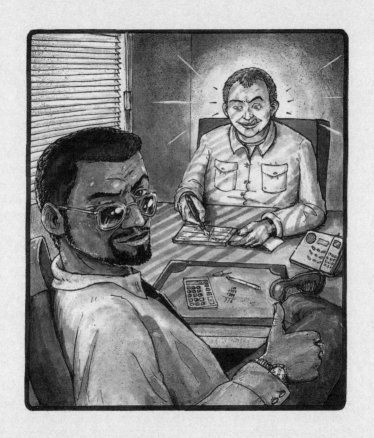

scam usually begins with you receiving an email or letter that purports to be from some Nigerian official or widow of a wealthy businessman who is sitting on an enormous pile of cash that has been legitimately acquired and needs help in moving it outside Nigeria. In return for that help the Gullible Groat will receive 20 per cent. But before the money can be released the Nigerian widow needs some cash to deal with the inevitable administration. If you are stupid enough to send money, you will then be asked for even more as various hitches and problems arise during the process of releasing the filthy lucre. Before you know it, you have given away tens of thousands of pounds and are still no nearer to getting the money. In fact, you never will. Some Americans are even duped into flying out to Nigeria where they are kidnapped, ransomed and even murdered. One elderly couple fell for this hook, line and sinker and ended up losing almost £100,000 in the process. The only reason why this type of scam works is the greed of the Gullible Groats involved. Another recent example involved an Admiral's son accused of running an international swindle from a former council maisonette. The guy running the scam netted some $2.2 million from gullible American Groats who were promised returns of excess of 400 per cent with no risk whatsoever. Of course none of the money sent by the Gullible Groats actually found its way into an investment vehicle. Instead it was used to pay off the fraudster's mortgage and buy him a new car. Then there were the people who believed that a television documentary that depicted a terrorist attack on London was actually real. The programme, *London Under Attack*, was a fictitious representation of what might happen if there was a chemical explosion in London. Viewers called in complaining that the programme was irresponsible and some moaned that their children had been in a blind panic believing what they were seeing was true. These fools who believed the programme obviously missed the clear sign on the bottom of the screen that stated the whole thing was purely fictional. If you have any of the following characteristics then you too might be a Gullible Groat: you want to get rich without working for it; you believe everything everyone tells you; you have a peanut for a brain and you would love to get involved with selling household products to your friends and family. If you display two or more of these qualities, seek help... now!

ANNOYANCE RATING

1 - Quite frankly, if you are stupid enough to fall for the various scams out there, then you deserve everything you get. The Nigerians are quite rightly scornful of how easily dumb Westerners fall for such obvious ploys and even legitimise their actions by saying that they are reparations for slavery. I actually think that Gullible Groats are not annoying at all and, if anything, are very amusing because they are so utterly stupid.

RARITY

5 – Gullible Groats are not as rare as we would expect. Although there is the only the occasional news article about some unsuspecting idiot falling for a scam, there are plenty of people out there who will take what people tell them at face value and will get involved with pyramid selling and get-rich-quick schemes.

SEASONAL VARIATIONS

The nature of the human condition and our inbuilt irrationality means that the Gullible Groat will display **no seasonal behaviours**. Such people are easy to fleece all year round and don't have the intelligence to snap out of it.

AVOIDANCE|REVENGE STRATEGIES

1. Never get involved with schemes that are designed to make you very rich very quickly.

2. Become a deep cynic and never believe anything anyone tells you. They are all liars, after all.

3. Go on a true confession programme like *Trisha* and discuss how your addiction to pyramid selling lost you your house, your marriage and your children.

4. Set up a scheme that involves selling tent pegs and radio-controlled donuts. Produce a brochure with some tacky pictures and endorsements from members of the scheme. Before you know it you'll be sitting on a huge pile of cash and a few dozen law suits.

5. Suggest the Gullible Groat gets a frontal lobotomy.

☐ Tick here when you have spotted the Gullible Groat

RATE THE
GULLIBLE GROAT'S
ANNOYANCE

The Hobo

Down and outs, bums, tramps or beggars – however we choose to refer to them, it seems that every town and city deserves at least half a dozen of them. The Hobos, as I prefer to call them, are a public nuisance. Of course we should feel sorry for their predicament and worry about how society allows these people to fall onto such hard times. However, they do have this tendency to make you feel nervous. Hobos have a number of characteristics that set them aside from the other folk in society, including:

- A tendency to congregate around park benches, shopping centres and underpasses where they consume bottles of meths or cider, stagger around drunk and get in other people's way. One group used to camp out under the Bullring in London, which was colloquially known as Cardboard City. They would have bonfires to keep them warm, the local authority would clean the site once a month and a soup van would pull up twice a day: a real home from home. In the end this was replaced with the Imax Cinema.
- Being somewhat smelly and dishevelled which, of course, should come as no surprise. After all, spending a couple of days camping anywhere has much the same effect.
- Ensconcing themselves on busy high streets and major thoroughfares so that you can't help but pass them. They sit on pieces of cardboard, cover themselves with blankets and take on a glum expression, a bit like a sad old dog. When you pass they will say, "Spare any loose change, please?" All of this is designed to make you feel bad enough to pass them a few pence. Some recognise that the standard mantra doesn't work and adopt more fanciful refrains such as "Can you spare me some change so that I can buy some whisky? Well, it was worth a try wasn't it?" Of course, it has the same success rate – zero.

- Dreaming up a wide range of excuses in order to dupe their victims. For example, I heard of one chap who at the time of the first Gulf War would approach people and wax lyrical about how he had absconded from the air force because he was a conscientious objector. Of course he hadn't. Another tactic, which I have to admit has fooled me only the once, is the "I'm sorry to disturb you, but I need a train fare to get back to Cambridge. I'm a student and here is the telephone number of my tutor which you can ring if you don't believe me…" routine. Naturally, all this spiel is enough to convince you to part with your money.

One guy told me about the time when he was walking past a Hobo on the way to the post office. As he walked past this unkempt old man, he noticed that he had a bottle of booze in his hand (of course) and was shouting some incomprehensible bollocks. He also noticed that the tramp's genitals were exposed. Anyway, a few minutes later as he was leaving the post office, he saw the tramp being dragged away by a couple of police officers. At the same time the tramp was busy urinating, leaving a trail of pee along the pavement. He was, of course, still churning out the incomprehensible bollocks. If you happen to work in a major conurbation, you tend to see the same Hobos day in, day out. This adds to the general feeling of Groundhog Day as you pass the same guy in the same location with his hand outstretched every single morning. I am sure you, as I do, try to alter your route when faced with this soul-destroying reminder of the monotony of daily life. Finally, it appears that being a Hobo is now fashionable with stressed-out executives. For £150, the high-flyer can spend a weekend sleeping rough on the streets. The fad, which started in America (where else?), involves not washing for five days beforehand, wearing old clothes and shoes, spending the days scavenging for food and the nights tucked up in some grimy hostel. The next time you see a Hobo lying around, it would be advisable to do a double take, as the person to whom you might be giving some cash to might really be running a global pharmaceutical company.

ANNOYANCE RATING

7 – Most Hobos are annoying because they manage to make you feel pity for their predicament whilst at the same time making your blood boil because they are invading your privacy. It is this combination that makes them so irritating as on one hand you want to ignore them and pretend they don't exist, whilst on the other, they make it impossible for you to walk by without noticing them. Groups of Hobos are especially annoying because they can be intimidating enough for you to find alternative and hence more circuitous routes to your destination.

RARITY

2 – Thankfully, compared to the general population, the number of Hobos is actually very small. Most towns have a few, whilst cities field a couple of hundred or so. Social Services and the police try to do their bit by taking them off the street and forcing them into hostels. However with the fragmentation of society and the general coldness people feel towards their fellow human beings, don't be surprised to see a few more over the coming years. After all, it won't be long before we are awash with students who have to become tramps to avoid paying their student loans.

SEASONAL VARIATIONS

Although the Hobo needs to eek out a living all year round, you will see less of them during the winter when additional hostel space will be made available. You will see more of them in **summer** when the days are long and the opportunity to gain some extra income from unsuspecting tourists is too enticing.

AVOIDANCE/REVENGE STRATEGIES

1. Avoid towns, cities and any major conurbations.

2. Give the Hobo a copy of *Hard Times* by Charles Dickens.

3. Look sincere and pass them by with a sad look on your face. If it helps, why not sniff an onion as you do to induce some tears?

4. Pass them the telephone number for the *Big Issue* which will help them pull themselves out of the gutter.

5. Cover yourself in dirt, sit next to them and see if you can earn more from begging than you do in the office.

☐ Tick here when you have spotted the Hobo

RATE THE **HOBO'S** ANNOYANCE

The Killjoy

There are people who have been put onto this planet to stop others from enjoying themselves. In the workplace we have witnessed the inexorable rise of political correctness and the increasing levels of petty officialdom designed to eliminate any sense of fun. But what of public life? Well, you could be mistaken in thinking that the 1930s chancellor of Germany is alive and well from all the Killjoys out there, doing their very best to ruin our free time. Like their office-based friends, the Killjoys will create all manner of obstacles to prevent us from having fun. The classic Killjoy is the petty official who, by virtue of their position, can introduce ridiculous rules and regulations to keep the general population in check. These are the people who will never bend the rules and will never grant you any flexibility, let alone freedom, in their interpretation. Indeed, if they had it their way, you would be under house arrest. Killjoys will work for local councils, as receptionists in doctor's surgeries, as tradesmen who fear petty officials and as, of course, our friends the Traffic Wardens. I was told of some chap who had bought a large house on the edge of a village and during the process of changing its aesthetics erected a brick wall and wrought iron gates. This made the house look like those you find in Beverly Hills. Unfortunately for the owner, someone in the village informed the planners and within a few weeks of completing the work, probably at great expense, he had to rip it all down again. There is a lesson here, of course, and that is never to cross the Killjoy. Other types of Killjoy with a more sinister undertone include the security guard and bouncer. The former will walk around shopping malls poking a nose into other peoples' business, telling them that they can't take their bikes through the centre or pulling them up for littering, whilst the latter will stop anybody they feel like from getting into bars and nightclubs. They will say such things as "You can't come in here with those trainers on" and then proceed to beat

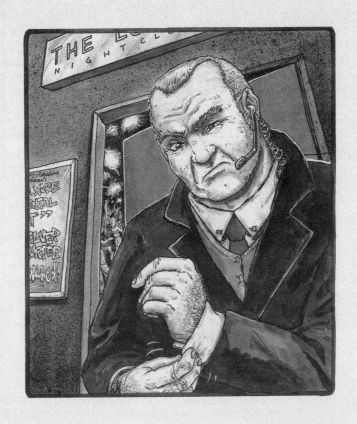

the shit out of you when you try. A chap who liked to take in the odd visit to lap dancing clubs was getting friendly with one of the dancers. Nothing serious, you understand, just a conversation about existentialism. Anyway, the bouncer rushed over and shouted at the guy, "Keep back from the merchandise!" "But I've done nothing wrong," replied the punter, explaining what he and "the merchandise" had been talking about. This was not sufficient to deter the bouncer from picking him by the scruff of the neck and ejecting him from the club. He then pursued the luckless man down the street swearing, threatening him and telling him never to come back. The problem was that the bouncer didn't understand what existentialism was and actually believed the guy was arranging some additional services of a sexual nature. Still, being a bouncer doesn't exactly require much in the cranium department apart from the ability to grunt, swear and coordinate your fists. Other examples of Killjoys having fun in their own special way include the following:

* In Louisiana it is now illegal to show any part of a G-string in public. Those people who contravene this essential piece of legislation will face up to six months in jail. The law states that anyone found exposing skin or intimate clothing below their trousers could be fined $500 or jailed.
* The local council that stipulated that punters at an adult club should remain at least three foot away from the strippers. As the owner pointed out, not only was this impossible to enforce without the use of a tape measure but as soon as one of the gentlemen visiting the club leaned forward, the new regulation would be broken. What's more, how would the short-sighted guy cope?
* A swimming club has been banned from training sessions at a public pool because the swimmers were making "too many waves" which were apparently unsettling elderly swimmers. The club is now only allowed to train its members individually.
* In Massachusetts it is illegal to sport a goatee beard unless you have permission and pay a fee. I reckon this is an excellent idea and should be introduced as quickly as possible in the UK.

ANNOYANCE RATING

7 - Killjoys naturally score highly on the annoyance scale because they crush our fun. You can't do anything these days without some trumped-up official informing you that you can't do this, that or the other. I can understand that we need to be kept in check for some things, but not everything. The Killjoy is someone who does not appreciate personal freedom.

RARITY

6 – Despite the massive increase in nanny-state regulations that inform us of what we can and cannot do, the Killjoy is not as common as we think. However, over time I am sure that the ranks of petty officialdom and the burgeoning private armies of the security companies will make the Killjoy far more common, but certainly not any more popular.

SEASONAL VARIATIONS

The Killjoy will be out in force **most of the year.** You will undoubtedly spot more of them at the weekends and during the summer when there are more people to control and upset.

AVOIDANCE|REVENGE STRATEGIES

1. When confronted by a Killjoy do whatever they say as this avoids any problems.

2. Do everything under the cover of darkness.

3. When accosted by a Killjoy pretend to be deaf, blind or an overseas visitor. Eventually they will get tired of trying to explain to you what you've done wrong and leave you alone.

4. Start a Givejoy movement that is designed to counter the petty officialdom that is wrecking the country. Be careful not to give the impression you are offering personal services, though...

5. Get a gang together and walk up to the Killjoy and chant something like "Killjoy, Killjoy, you've got no friends and everyone hates you".

☐ Tick here when you have spotted the Killjoy

> RATE THE
> *KILLJOY'S*
> ANNOYANCE

The Ladette

*E*quality has finally reached every part of society. For a long, long time, successive governments have worried themselves to death over the young men who wasted their lives getting drunk, brawling, vomiting and generally making a bloody nuisance of themselves. Not any more. Women have now got into the act. Welcome to the Ladette. The Ladettes are usually in their twenties, thirties and occasionally their forties, although the forty-year-old Ladette is often known as the Slapper. The Ladette is a woman who has adopted many of the attitudes and behaviours of her male counterpart including a preference for hard drinking, swearing, confrontation, sexual pushiness, vomiting, fornication, burping, scratching her crack and violence. This last aspect of Ladettes' behaviour is particularly entertaining. One chap witnessed two fighting in a car park. It was amazing how violent they were: pulling each other's hair, biting and clawing faces. They were fighting over some man they had both been sleeping with, but not at the same time (poor guy). According to one survey, the typical Ladette will fritter away the weekend clubbing all night and sleeping all day (and who with?). One particular trait of the Ladette is their obsession with shagging which is clearly evident when on holiday. The typical Ladette will save all her cash from her job in the local chip shop to travel with her mates to places like Ayia Napa and Faliraki. Once there the Ladettes will party every night, go on boozy rampages shagging everything in sight and baring their tits to the local police, which normally gets them into trouble. Their primary objective is to fast track their holiday romance, which can be translated into the need to get laid as many times as possible before returning to their boring lives. Most of this shagging is performed in a drunken stupor. Groups of Ladettes will stand at one end of the street shouting, "What do we want?

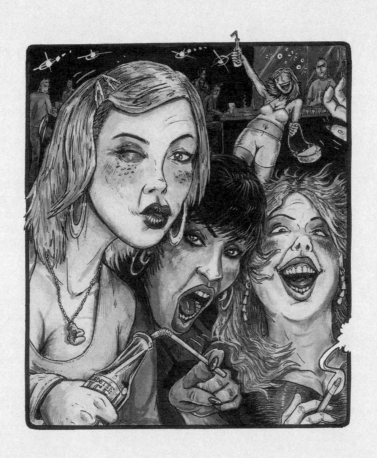

Willies! How do we want them? Hard!" The spotty boys at the other end duly oblige. Ladette behaviour has extended into two main areas:

- **Hen Nights,** where a bunch of women will descend on a bar, restaurant or nightclub to celebrate the last days of freedom of the poor woman who is getting hitched. The bride-to-be will often wear a veil (so you can spot who she is) and the whole group will usually sport T-shirts or badges indicating that they are on a mission. Now this mission might entail getting wrecked, greasing up a stripogram or running amok, but whatever it is you can be guaranteed some amusement. One restaurant banned hen nights after a group crossed the boundaries of decency by mimicking sex acts in front of other guests.
- **Girl Gangs,** who walk around town abusing their fellow citizens, shoplifting and, if in America, shooting people. One particular bunch of girls targeted designer shops. Whilst one or two would abuse the assistants by aggressively ordering them to fetch shoes and handbags, their colleagues in crime would help themselves to huge quantities of designer goods.

One woman had to share a journey with a group of antipodean Ladettes on the way to a beach party. The group consisted of something in the region of ten young ladies all shouting, swearing and telling tales of how worse for wear they were the night before and how they were going to get plenty of grog down their necks before going out on the pull. It was f**k this and f**k that as they looked around to confirm they were getting the appropriate looks from the more sensible people around them. Of course, with all this binge drinking, most Ladettes will be suffering from end-stage liver disease by the time they are in their late thirties. Perhaps when they get old they will be called Grannyettes and they'll be dawdling round shopping centres gobbing on young mothers with babies.

ANNOYANCE RATING

6 – This all depends on whether you think it is great to see a bunch of young women pissed, throwing-up and behaving like blokes. If you do, then you are probably going to have a great time. There are people who find the Ladette's beer-swilling antics a tad boring and unsophisticated, although much of this is probably down to jealousy.

RARITY

9 – The number of Ladettes has increased dramatically since they became popular during the 1990s. With increased levels of independence and more money from better paying jobs, it's payback time for the years spent in feminist or chauvinistic repression. It's time to party, vomit and put it about a bit. Female hedonism is clearly in, and here to stay.

SEASONAL VARIATIONS

Friday and Saturday nights are always a good time to spot the Ladette. Ladettes will also come out in force during the summer months when there are more men to pull, they can drink outside and generally strip down to make their bodies, at least, more attractive. You will also spot the Ladette on her hen night, especially during the **summer months** when weddings are all the rage.

AVOIDANCE|REVENGE STRATEGIES

1. Avoid all the obvious haunts of the Ladette: the pub, nightclub, beaches in summer and dodgy holiday resorts.

2. Always be wary of any group of women staggering down the street shouting "Get your todger out". And, for you men among my readers, a tip: don't.

3. Dress up as a priest and lecture them on Sodom and Gomorrah.

4. Stand on street corners dishing out free condoms, sick bags and STD testing kits.

5. Test just how much of a Ladette one is by asking her to match you pint for pint and shag for shag.

☐ Tick here when you have spotted the Ladette

RATE THE
LADETTE'S
ANNOYANCE

The Movie-Going Moron

I am not sure how many new films are released every year, but I guess they must number in the hundreds. Most are terrible B-movies or that made for television trash that finds itself onto our small screen, but the ones we get to see at the cinema are at least half decent and often blockbusters. I have always loved going to the cinema. Now given that a significant proportion of us likes to go to the cinema we should expect to meet a few deviants from time to time. Such people are known as Movie-Going Morons. The Movie-Going Moron is someone who refuses to follow the standard conventions associated with watching a film. As a child I don't recall that many of them, as an adolescent I saw a few, but as an adult I see way too many. The Movie-Going Moron comes in a variety of guises including:

- The **Mobile Muppet** who insists on using a phone whilst in the cinema. Now, I thought the whole point of going to the movies was to enjoy the film, not ruin other people's enjoyment. But no, this is clearly not the case. The Mobile Muppet will ring friends and family and give them blow-by-blow accounts of the movie. Surely these people should have come themselves if they were that interested? Others text their way through the film and there are even those who will take business calls. It's just another example of the type of cretin whose life can only be given meaning through the mobile phone. New York is hoping to introduce a ban on the use of mobile phones in cinemas, where phones and pagers typically go off every two minutes.
- The **What's the Plot**, who has to ask insane questions throughout the film, like "What's Frodo doing up that mountain?" I am sure if they were sitting next to the film's director they would receive a cogent answer, but given that it's their granny or husband they are sitting with, how on earth do they expect them to give an answer, let alone a sensible one? The whole point of the plot is for

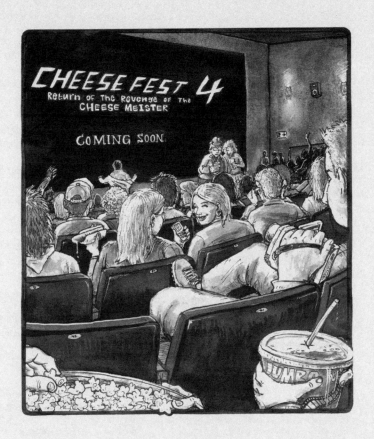

you to figure it out for yourself and enjoy the spectacle, not ask stupid questions. In some instances people have been known to bring in laser pointers and use these to point to various parts of the scene and then talk loudly about what they are pointing at.

- The **Muncher and Litterer** will buy popcorn, sweets, nachos, coke, crisps, hotdogs and all sorts of fast food crap and then eat it loudly during the film. As someone who likes to purchase vast quantities of popcorn for my kids and myself I can see just how annoying it is for those around me. The crunching, gulping, swallowing and rustling is enough to drive anyone mad, plus the mess most people leave behind makes the cinema resemble a war zone.

- The **Chatterbox**, who insists on holding conversations throughout the film. What's surprising about these is that they are usually about domestic issues and other topics totally unrelated to the movie. Why on earth can't they discuss them over a coffee outside?

- The **Weirdo**, who behaves in an unconventional way whilst in the cinema. For example, there are some people who love going to the adult cinemas you find in places like Soho or parts of Amsterdam. They are known as the Brown Mac Brigade. Their simple objective is to play pocket billiards whilst watching couples cavorting on the screen. I was told of one guy who was watching 91/2 Weeks, a film full of perversions but which was screened in "alternative cinemas" which allowed the general public to watch it without the need to pass loads of sex shops. He wore a long mac and at various points in the movie would rustle around his groin area and then dash to the toilets to return a few minutes later. He would salivate and lick his lips at any scene that was remotely suggestive.

My personal pet hates in the cinema are very tall people who will always sit in front of you, people who constantly ask stupid questions and the weak-bladdered, who are always getting up, pushing past you and going to the toilet.

ANNOYANCE RATING

9 – The Movie-Going Moron rates very highly on the annoyance scale. If you have paid good money to see a film you expect to be able to see it in silence. So when you get a succession of idiots chewing, talking and phoning throughout the "entertainment" it's enough to make you see red, which some people do.

RARITY

7 – Unfortunately, with the ubiquitous nature of mobile telephony, the desire to bump up profits through the sale of popcorn, nachos and other noisy consumables and the inconsiderate nature of people in general, the Movie-Going Moron is surprisingly common.

SEASONAL VARIATIONS

Although the Movie-Going Moron will be with us **all year**, you will be able to spot more of them during the summer and at Christmas when the blockbusters are released.

AVOIDANCE|REVENGE STRATEGIES

1. Only ever go to the cinema at obscure times when most people are at work.

2. Wait until films come out on DVD and watch them in the comfort of your own living room.

3. Seek to have mobile phones banned from cinemas.

4. Make as much noise as you can by bringing in a personal stereo and mobile phone. In addition buy as much popcorn as you can and eat it with your mouth open.

5. Arm yourself with night vision goggles and a sniper rifle. Whenever a Movie-Going Moron disturbs your enjoyment, take them out with a head shot.

☐ Tick here when you have spotted the Movie-Going Moron

RATE THE
*MOVIE-GOING
MORON'S
ANNOYANCE*

The Nightmare Neighbour

GENERAL CHARACTERISTICS

Many years ago you could leave your front door wide open during the day and unlocked at night without any concerns for your safety or indeed for your property (if you had any, of course). Life was simple and safe; neighbours would pop in to chew the fat and share the odd cup of tea with you, and your children would play on the sun-drenched streets during the summer. In this day and age your door is firmly bolted to keep out all the scumbags who are trying to sell you things, and your children are under strict supervision to keep them away from all the nutters and perverts wandering the streets. These days you have to contend with the Nightmare Neighbour who is out to destroy any sense of serenity you might have or, indeed, desire. Here is a small sample of the types of Nightmare Neighbour you might come across and seek to avoid:

- The **Boundary Bigot**, who is obsessed about the boundary between their property and yours. Such people will go to extraordinary lengths to ensure that their property covers the exact proportions laid out in its registration documents. And, be warned, if necessary they will take you to court over a sliver of grass barely two centimetres wide. What's worse is when they decide to plant fast growing conifers to delineate the boundary and cut out all your light to leave you in near darkness. Such Leylandii Losers, as they are called, should be pulped along with their trees. themselves.
- The **Disco Bum No Mark** is typified by a poor taste in music coupled with an inability to turn the volume down. Disco Bum No Marks normally sleep during the day and play music all night, generally at full volume. They will never heed your requests to turn their music down and the only way to shut them up is to smash their doors down and take an axe to their sound systems.

- The **Nutcase**, who should be sectioned and put out of harm's way. One woman used to terrorise an entire neighbourhood. She was a squat-faced witch who was built like an breezeblock; she was drunk most of the time and would apparently drink a bottle of whisky for breakfast. Her favourite trick was to beat up other mothers in the playground which was usually preceded by "What are you f***ing looking at?" as a advance warning.

- The **Nosey Know-All,** who will lean over your fence and engage you in mindless conversations about the weather, what you are doing and absolutely anything so long as it involves you in some kind of discussion. One such child would constantly pester her neighbours by whining "What you doing, man?" constantly. Day in, day out she would stand at the fence, which was low enough for her to see over, and chant those magic words. In the end the woman next door shouted at her "What the f**k does it look like I'm doing?" and she fled.

- The **Municipal Dump**, who has no concept of tidiness, cleanliness or even neighbourliness. The Municipal Dump's house and garden are a rubbish tip. They will leave household appliances to rot in the front garden, along with rusty old cars and pieces of furniture. Over time the house will turn to rubble, the windows will fall out and the garden will take on the appearance of the Amazonian Jungle. The stench from such neighbours, especially during the summer months, is nothing short of disgusting.

Recently we heard of a woman who on balmy summer evenings would strip off, strip her companion off and have sex in her garden jacuzzi which was strategically placed so that all her neighbours could see and, of course, hear what was going on. She revelled in making it obvious she was enjoying herself with her latest and longest stallion. I also heard of three students who hated the sitting tenant who lived beneath them so much that they would perform simulated sex on the floor above to annoy him and smash a hammer against the wall in order to dislodge the plaster which would fall down the cavity. Bloody students.

ANNOYANCE RATING

10 – For those who have to suffer the inconsiderate behaviour of Nightmare Neighbours there can be nothing worse. Driven to distraction, mental breakdown and occasionally physical violence, these poor people deserve some respite. The problem is that it is almost impossible to rid yourself of Nightmare Neighbours without the use of a shotgun. In the end you are the one that has to move.

RARITY

6 – With the town planners having a preference for huge housing estates, the number of Nightmare Neighbours is on the increase. With so little greenbelt available, people are being forced into ever-closer proximity with their fellow human beings. Statistically, therefore, at least three years of the average person's life will be ruined by the actions of their Nightmare Neighbours.

SEASONAL VARIATIONS

None. Unfortunately the Nightmare Neighbour will be with you until either you move away or die, or they move away or die. You can always hope.

AVOIDANCE|REVENGE STRATEGIES

1. Live on an island surrounded by water which is only accessible by helicopter.

2. Invite the producers of *A Life of Grime* or *Neighbours from Hell* to film your estate.

3. Buy a bulldozer and raze the Nightmare Neighbour's house to the ground.

4. Cut off their electricity.

5. Model yourself on Charles Bronson and become a local vigilante taking on the Nightmare Neighbour in the same way he did in *Death Wish*.

☐ Tick here when you have spotted the Nightmare Neighbour

RATE THE
**NIGHTMARE
NEIGHBOUR'S**
ANNOYANCE

The Noisy Git

GENERAL CHARACTERISTICS

Toxic noise. That's the phrase associated with noises that can destroy and irreversibly damage our hearing. Unfortunately our environment is an increasingly noisy one. Most of us can cope with some noise but there are those in society who make so much racket that you can't hear yourself think, let alone hear other people talk. Such people are known as the Noisy Gits. The number of complaints about noisy neighbours in particular continues to grow; last year there were almost 250,000. Amplified music accounts for 76 per cent of all complaints and next on the list comes the barking dog. Dogs that are left at home all day whilst their owner, often a Dogmess Merchant, is at work are especially annoying. They will often bark for hours on end. New York has introduced a ban on barking dogs, a great idea which I hope catches on here. Probably the best way to silence them is to put them down. But it is not only the inconsiderate jerks we live next door to who drive us nuts with all the noise they make. Our hatred of noise stems from a huge variety of sources, including:

* Defective burglar and car alarms. Because these alarms are meant to be heard they are incredibly loud and difficult to ignore especially if they go off at night. House alarms are notorious for going off whenever they like which infuriates neighbours and police alike. Car alarms, although annoying, are rarely investigated. People are so used to these things going off that they would rather the bloody vehicles were stolen. Alarms raise blood pressure, increase stress hormones and apparently lead to "learned helplessness" in children... whatever that is.

- Boomboxes in youths' cars. These enormous stereo systems take up the entire back seat of the car, which is usually driven around towns, cities and especially seaside resorts throughout the day and night. The noise is so loud that they can be heard up to half a mile in each direction. In fact one such boombox claims to chuck out a whopping 175 decibels; this 48,000 watt system is eight times louder than a 747 jet.
- Lawnmowers, leaf blowers, chainsaws and other garden equipment which are all incredibly loud and which for some strange reason are only ever used on a Sunday morning when you are trying to have a well-deserved lie in. Most of these contraptions whine like a dentist's drill with the same mind-numbing effect. Leaf blowers are a particular scourge in America where people will use them to dry their lawn after it has rained, clear their driveway of dead bodies from drive-by shootings and clean their windscreens. At 110 decibels it's no wonder they drive people mad.
- Mobile phones and their inconsiderate users who shout into the handset. For more on that see Pains on Trains.
- Transport. Whether it is trains, trams, cars or planes you can almost guarantee that, wherever you are, there will be noise from one form of transport or another. Living near an airport is particularly disturbing.

People can clearly get extremely upset with those who disturb their tranquillity. Women apparently turn to unhealthy snacks and junk food when stress is brought on by noise. Men just get violent. There are some novel solutions to the problem of the Noisy Git. A bunch of college students in Connecticut who failed to comply with a noise abatement order were forced to listen to opera and in Louisiana offenders are made to attend a three-hour music appreciation event of their least favourite music, which in most cases is Country and Western (which doesn't surprise me. Maybe they should be forced to do line dancing too). In Nebraska the owners of boomboxes that can be heard more than fifty feet away spend three months in jail.

ANNOYANCE RATING

9 – Noisy Gits rate highly on the annoyance scale and although we may harp on and complain about their inconsiderate behaviour, we should remember the biblical saying, "He that is without sin among you, let him first cast a stone." We are all guilty. It's not just our neighbours who are mowing their lawns, it's us too. It's not just the Chavs with their boomboxes who play loud music whilst driving, we do too. So before you start to get angry just remember that you are probably a Noisy Git as well.

RARITY

10 – Modern day existence brings with it a huge array of devices that make incredible amounts of noise. Couple this with a high level of inconsiderate behaviour and you have a veritable noise boom on your hands. Being a Noisy Git is a popular pastime.

SEASONAL VARIATIONS

The **summer** will always bring out more Noisy Gits than normal. Open windows and sunshine means that you'll hear more music, more boomboxes, more dogs, more lawnmowers... more everything.

AVOIDANCE|REVENGE STRATEGIES

1. Move well away from any source of noise. Perhaps the best place to be might be next to a decommissioned nuclear power station.

2. Plug up your ears and soundproof your home.

3. Buy a decibel meter and record the readings. Use this as evidence when you take the Noisy Git to court.

4. Drive around town with an unfeasibly large and powerful loudhailer proclaiming the end of noise pollution.

5. Arm yourself with riot foam and attack anyone who so much as whispers.

☐ Tick here when you have spotted the Noisy Git

RATE THE
NOISY GIT'S
ANNOYANCE

The Parking Police

Attempting to park these days is a Herculean task. With over 26 million cars on the road, it's bad enough trying to avoid all the Dreadful Drivers, let alone find somewhere to leave your car for a few minutes. However, we all detest the inconsiderate driver who parks a car on a blind bend, at a road junction, in the middle of the road, straddling two parking bays, in the disabled spot when they are able bodied and especially in front of our house. Of course, when we are parking, we believe we have the right to park wherever we choose; after all, we pay our road tax. To combat these bad behaviours we have an army of Parking Police whose sole job in life is to deter you and I from parking where the hell we like. The Parking Police have the power to make our lives a misery. They come in four basic forms:

- The **Cowboy Clampers**, who will ride into town, immobilise your car and then demand extortionate amounts of cash from you in order to unclamp it. Most are travellers, live off a diet of kebabs and cheep booze and cruise around towns and cities looking out for their next victim.
- The **Wicked Wardens**, who would issue a ticket to an ambulance given half a chance. For them, cutting motorists any slack is a sign of weakness. Indeed, the more tickets they can issue, the more kudos they receive.
- The **Tow-Away Toerags**, who will load your car onto the back of a bloody great lorry and impound it in some remote yard that you will first have to locate before trying to find your car.
- The **Private Pouncers**, who are employed by train stations, hospitals and municipal car parks and will hover around your car and issue a fine as soon as you fail to pay for a ticket.

With unending pressure to raise more income for the government and the increased used of underhand tactics, the Parking Police have become the number one hate guys on our roads today. Their sinister approaches to extorting money include:

- Telling drivers that it is OK to park in a certain place when asked and, once they have, clamping or issuing them with a ticket after the driver walks away.
- Deliberately targeting people they don't like the look of, irrespective of whether they have parked illegally or not.
- Clamping hearses (with dead bodies in), police cars (whilst the police were attempting to apprehend suspects), and mothers (who are rushing their children to surgeries)
- Impounding cars, failing to tell the owners that they have been taken away and then letting their kids drive them.
- Demanding wedding rings, gold teeth and sexual favours in order to release clamped vehicles. In extreme cases, they have even held children ransom to expedite payment.

One guy went into town to drop a package off at a local business. He had been gone less than a minute and on his return he saw a Wicked Warden hovering by his car like a bee around a honey pot. "How long have you been parked here, sir?" he was asked. "Less than a minute," the chap replied. "And who are you trying to kid, sir? Your bonnet is cold. You must have been here for at least two hours." "No, I live locally and I have been here all of two minutes." "I'm sorry, but I don't believe you." The warden then issued a ticket. You see, the Parking Police do not have a considerate or humane bone in them. No longer content with fining people for illegal parking, the Parking Police have recently turned their attention to box junctions. Under sweeping new legislation, they can now issue fines for any motorist that ignores right-turn bans, abuses bus lanes, or performs illegal U-turns. It's a Parking Police charter with thousands more entering the ranks of the neo-attendants hell-bent on persecuting innocent drivers. I feel a protest coming on.

ANNOYANCE RATING

5 – This all depends. If you know you are breaking the law by parking illegally you should expect the full weight of it to descend on you. However, if you believe you are parking legally, or if you are involved with an emergency, then the actions of the Parking Police are completely out of order. What really irritates are their underhand tactics, all of which are designed to maximise their revenue. Cowboy Clampers are even worse because they tend to operate outside the law and don't give a stuff about what they clamp, who they clamp and when they clamp.

RARITY

6 – Taken as a population, the combined masses of Cowboy Clampers and Wicked Wardens is significant. I am sure they must be as numerous as the rat population; in fact, I believe they are part of it. With more than ten million parking tickets issued every year, even the Pied Piper would be hard pressed to lead all the Parking Police into a swollen river.

SEASONAL VARIATIONS

None. The only time you will see less of the Parking Police is when everyone is tucked snugly up in their beds, with their cars on their drives or in their garages. Apart from then, Parking Police are over you like a rash.

AVOIDANCE|REVENGE STRATEGIES

1. Avoid the Parking Police by always parking legally.

2. Buy some false parking tickets and wheel clamps and set up your own business. All you need is a dodgy address and a mobile phone and, hey presto, you're on your way to making your first million.

3. Always keep a chainsaw in the boot of your car.

4. Construct a rat trap large enough to accommodate a human. Place it next to your illegally parked car, arm it and watch what happens from behind a nearby bush.

5. Put false number plates on your car and park wherever you want.

☐ Tick here when you have spotted the Parking Police

RATE THE
PARKING POLICE'S
ANNOYANCE

The Partygoer

GENERAL CHARACTERISTICS

Going to parties is normally a fun experience. It's an opportunity to let your hair down, sink a few drinks and perhaps get overly familiar with members of the opposite sex. The Partygoer lives off a succession of parties, be they of the student variety that often involves the obligatory wearing of togas (which from personal experience is incredibly dull) or the Celeb party which is organised by some "it girl" (surely missing an "sh"?) or socialite whom nobody actually likes but nonetheless has the useful function of planning good bashes. Youths love, and parents dread, the parties held at home. Such parties are typically organised when mum and dad are away on holiday. One such party included a guy chucking up over a girl as he French kissed her and the poor chap, whose house it was, attempting to vacuum up the vomit that had been left on his parents' beautiful red carpet. I was told of one party that was so well publicised by the guy who was running it that people were literally queuing up to gatecrash. The gatecrashers got so upset with having to queue, and with the fact that all the booze had been consumed by the earlier uninvited guests, that they started to throw bricks through the front windows. Eventually the police were called and the party brought to an abrupt halt. The irony of the whole thing was that the party was being held at a police house. In addition to the adolescent partygoers there are a number of others of which the following are the most common:

- The **Students** who will crush themselves into the front room of their digs and consume vast quantities of cheap booze. The whole objective is to get totally smashed so that they can come out with that classic student statement: "What did I get up to last night? I was sooo drunk I can't remember a thing, tell me I didn't do anything stupid…"

- The **Thirty-Somethings** who are holding onto their student days, thinking that they can still misbehave and act like immature prats. They love acting cool and listening to the same trendy music they did whilst at university.
- The **Forty-Somethings**, who are no longer capable of letting their hair down. They stand around uncomfortably, talking with near strangers about mundane day-to-day issues such as Peter's whooping cough or the price of bread. There is this awful need within the Forty-Something Partygoer to try and hold onto their youth, which can manifest itself in a number of ways. At one party a women decided it would be a great idea to show her knickers and breasts to fellow guests which didn't go down too well. Another variant is the wife-swapping party. This is a favourite of the suburban set, who prefer to take their neighbour's wife from behind than go wild on the dance floor.
- The **Celebs**, who will attend any function that gets their mugs in the media. Most tabloids and lifestyle magazines fall over themselves to include cheesy pictures of well-known and B-list Celebs posing at the latest society party. A huge commentary follows in which their Versace clothes are analysed as is who is, or is not, hanging off their arm.
- The **Charity Giver** who must be seen at all the major charity events of the year. As the whole objective of such events is to make lots of cash for the charity, only those who are willing to fork out a small fortune attend. So you'd expect to see the usual Celebs plus a handful of influential businessmen who want to demonstrate that they are not complete money-grabbing, self-serving bastards. Of course, none of us believe them because their entrance fees are paid by their company.

At the end of the party, the Partygoer can seen staggering down the street looking very much the worse for wear. Their beautiful evening wear or fancy dress outfit will be creased and covered in all sorts of things, which may include lipstick, food, alcohol and (as you might expect) vomit. In fact the Partygoer will be the origin of the many Pavement Pizzerias (read on) that litter our pavements in the morning.

ANNOYANCE RATING

6 – Partygoers are rarely annoying on the way to parties. It's whilst they are there and certainly when they are on the way home that they are at their most irritating. With loud voices, the occasional argument and fist fight, as well as the retching and splattering noises that come with the very drunk, it is almost impossible to sleep.

RARITY

4 – How common the Partygoer is will depend on where you live. If you happen to be in a town or city with a university you should expect to see plenty of students running amok and having a "wicked" time. If you happen to live in a sleepy retirement village it is safe to say that you will spot few if any Partygoers apart from the occasional undertaker who is beside himself at all the business he is getting. You'd also have to be eagle eyed to spot the Forty-Something Partygoer, but the Volvos parked up outside a house might be a dead giveaway as will the cowboy gait these people have when they have finished swapping their partners. As for the Celebs and Charity Givers, you only see them in the glossy magazines.

SEASONAL VARIATIONS

You will see plenty more Partygoers in the **run up to Christmas** and during the **summer months,** when they love to party outside. New Year is, of course, when they come out in force, a time when everyone pretends that 1 January will bring new hope and opportunity when, in fact, nothing changes.

AVOIDANCE/REVENGE STRATEGIES

1. Stay at home and build a matchstick replica of the Mary Rose.

2. Go to all the parties you can; that way you'll be part of the problem and won't be at all annoyed by the Partygoers.

3. Whenever there is a party next door or in your neighbourhood make an anonymous phone call to the police to get them to shut it down.

4. Pose as a paparazzi photographer and gatecrash all the celebrity and charity parties. The food is great and you can get autographs of all the rich and famous.

5. Organise a huge party to cater for every conceivable Partygoer. Once in full swing send in the Drugs Squad to search everyone for illegal substances.

☐ Tick here when you have spotted the Partygoer

RATE THE
PARTYGOER'S
ANNOYANCE

The Pensioner

The song *My Generation* by The Who had some wonderful lyrics in it directed at the old in society, but it's a shame that most of the band didn't comply with their most pointed phrase: "I hope I die before I get old." Old people or Pensioners, as they are generally called, are the fastest-growing cohort in western society and increasingly across the world. In fact, by 2030 Zimmer frames will outnumber pushchairs in the United States and there will be twice as many retired people than there are today. What is shocking about this statistic is that I will be one of them! The Pensioners, like all pains, believe they are not annoying. However, ask anyone below the age of fifty and you'd probably get an entirely different perspective. Pensioners clog up our roads, streets, shopping centres and, of course, our hospitals. Typical aspects of their lifestyle that grate on the young include:

- Thinking that just because they are Pensioners they should be afforded special privileges like cheap food, cheap transport, haircuts and holidays. Surely it should be the other way around, given that it is those in employment who have to pay for them all?
- Expecting sympathy. I heard of one Pensioner, who quite frankly didn't look a day over fifty, complaining to some debt-collecting company about how she was paying her credit card debt out of her pension. If she was stupid enough to get into debt knowing full well that she couldn't afford it, then it's her own fault – Pensioner or not.
- Being cantankerous and lacking many of the social skills we should expect of an ancient and supposedly wise member of society. It is well known that people begin to lose their ability to hold their tongue as they get older. Men and women alike will complain about

everything, go on about how discourteous people are and be short-tempered with everyone around them.

- Not being able to cope with modern life, either complaining that everything is changing too fast or obsessing about the good old days when life was simple and all you had to worry about were the Nazis dropping bombs on your home.

- Driving when they shouldn't. As we get older our reaction times slow considerably, which makes it harder to drive safely on our increasingly clogged-up roads. A 75-year-old woman was recently convicted of dangerous driving when she was travelling no more than five miles an hour on a busy road. She, like so many older drivers, was oblivious to her surroundings. Fortunately the police are about to introduce an "impairment-ometer", a hand-held device that will detect the slow reactions of the elderly driver in an effort to crack down on Pensioners who should not be on the road.

The one thing the Pensioner does have is oodles of time in which to do what the hell they like. This is fantastic, but why do they decide to do it when everyone else wants to? Take shopping, for example. During the week, they can pop to their local supermarket whenever they want, so why do they insist on going at the weekend? The same applies with the roads. During the working week, there are comparatively few cars on the road, especially after the morning and evening rush hours, so why do they persist on driving around on a Sunday afternoon? Pensioners are also very slow, taking a lot longer to perform even the simplest of tasks. Take paying for goods as a prime example. Whereas you or I might hand the shop assistant a five-pound note and wait for the change, the Pensioner will dig around in an oversized purse for hours in an attempt to offload their entire change collection onto the hapless shop assistant. This, as you'd expect, takes an absolute age. Interestingly there is a pensioner backlash amongst the baby boom generation, who are rejecting the notions of old age in favour of travel, taking up new sports and hobbies and washing more often. Are they bucking the trend or refusing to face up to the inevitable?

ANNOYANCE RATING
8 – Young people will always have major issues with Pensioners and so will find them annoying in the same way that they find the young irritating. I guess one of the principal reasons why Pensioners are perceived to be so annoying is because they get in the way of everyone else; we're always in such a terrible hurry these days.

RARITY
9 – Although Pensioners are no longer capable of breeding, they seem to be doing a bloody good job of increasing their numbers. Sure, we'll all get old and if we have saved enough during our working lives we might be able to enjoy what few years left we have before we turn to dust. But whilst we are young enough to do more than just dribble and smell of mince and wee should make the most of it. Before long we'll be joining the ranks of the infirm and mentally deranged.

SEASONAL VARIATIONS
None at all. Pensioners are with us every day of every week of every month of every year. The only time they are not around is when they have passed away.

AVOIDANCE|REVENGE STRATEGIES
1. Live in a developing nation, where people are still very young and there are very few, if any, Pensioners.

2. Always go out at night, as this is when most Pensioners will be tucked up in their beds watching their favourite soap opera.

3. Insist that the pensionable age is increased to 80. Mind you, the government has pretty much done this already.

4. Distribute copies of the TV series *Grumpy Old Men*, together with the associated book.

5. Bring in compulsory euthanasia.

☐ Tick here when you have spotted the Pensioner

RATE THE **PENSIONERS** ANNOYANCE

The Plane Pain

Any book about the painful people you meet in public must not ignore the whole plane thing. In the same way that trains create an environment from which you cannot escape, planes do the same. I actually enjoy travelling by plane… well, so long as it's not long-haul in cattle class. Despite what class you are flying in, there are all manner of people whom you would love to avoid, but know you can't. As soon as the Plane Pain sits next to you, you know you are in for a terrible journey. The worst offenders in the air are:

- The **Business-Class Boozers**, who tank themselves up on free champagne and other alcoholic delights and then spend the rest of the flight trying to get off with the stewardess and female passengers. One chap I heard of was a classic Business-Class Boozer who not only walked around the cabin engaging his fellow passengers in mindless conversation, but also propositioned the stewardess. She lent over him and said in a rather loud voice, "I do hope you're not one of those drunk passengers." The guy, suitably chastised, sat back in his seat and promptly went to sleep.
- The **Berserkers**, who will go mad in the cabin attacking airline staff, fellow passengers and anyone who gets in their way. I can certainly understand why someone would go mad on a long-haul charter flight because there is barely enough room for a midget let alone someone approaching average height. Only recently did I hear of a man going berserk and forcing an inbound flight from the US to make an unscheduled stop in Ireland for him to be taken away. Apparently it took six attempts for him to be subdued and during the fracas no one was allowed to leave their seats unless they were desperate for a leak. At least he didn't have explosives in his shoe.

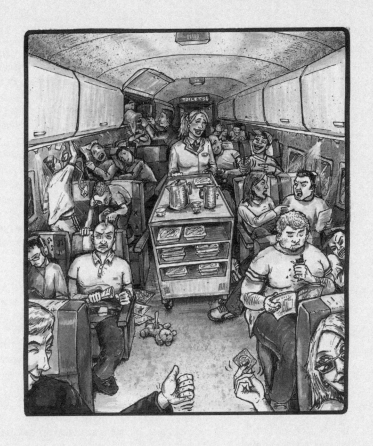

- The **Uncontrollable Children** who, through no fault of their own, find themselves on flights way before they ought to. Why on earth do parents insist on bringing a three-week-old baby on a flight to America? It screams, gurgles, vomits and poos its nappy, which is then changed on its mother's lap. Camping would be a better option for everyone, especially for whoever is sitting next to the mother at this point. Then there are the young kids who can barely sit still for two minutes without fidgeting, asking their mothers for something, or telling the whole cabin that they feel sick.
- The **Gigantic Gits**, who will make your trip a misery. These people take up more than their fair share of seat space and reduce the baggage allowance for all of us because they weigh more then the suitcases for a family of four. My wife and I had the joy of sitting next to an enormous woman on a tortuous flight to Thailand. The woman was so large that when it came to mealtime, she would rest the tray on her oversized breasts and lick the food from the plate. It was disgusting. What made the whole experience so unbearable for my wife was that she was feeling pretty poorly and the spectacle of this vast woman consuming her food was enough to tip her over the edge.

Some Plane Pains can't help it, but that doesn't stop them being pains. A woman was travelling with her companion to Florida one Easter. As they settled into their seats, looking forward to the next two weeks, a group of people got onto the plane. At first they appeared completely normal. As the plane taxied along the runway and readied itself for takeoff, they heard this "F***! W***! C***!". They thought the person concerned was directing his abuse at them. When they turned around to see who it was it was clear that the poor chap was suffering from Tourette's Syndrome. Every now and then he would also don a white face mask and spit into it whilst swearing uncontrollably; the next seven hours seemed to last forever. Anyway, the holiday came and went and, in order to avoid the poor guy on the return journey, the ladies upgraded. As they settled into their seats, hoping to get some sleep on the flight home, which was at night, who should appear? Yes, you've guessed it: Mr. Tourette's.

ANNOYANCE RATING

6 – Flying should be fun, especially if you are going on holiday. Well, it would be if you had the flight to yourself. It's bad enough having to sit in cramped conditions, but things get much worse when you are next to someone you would rather see tortured than spend nine hours with. One especially annoying feature of flying is the fight once the plane lands. What is it with people that they feel they need to push and shove as they get their hand luggage from the overhead compartments before the doors have opened? Do they really think it is going to make that much difference? And do they think they will get their luggage any faster?

RARITY

8 – With so many of us flying these days and with it being cheaper than chips we should expect to bump into plenty of Plane Pains. Until the oil runs out, we won't be able to escape them. Planes, trains…blimey, there really is no escape!

SEASONAL VARIATIONS

You will see a lot more of the Plane Pain during the **summer** months and any **school holiday** when everyone will be trying to get away from the wet and windy weather back home. You will see many more Business-Class Boozers during **any economic boom** and far fewer during any recession when they will travel on low-cost airlines along with all the Chavs.

AVOIDANCE|REVENGE STRATEGIES

1. Go by boat.

2. Fly first class. It's great; you get a huge personal space and have three stewardesses to tend to your every need. What's more, you even get a pair of pyjamas.

3. Refuse to sit next to children, fat people, drunks, perverts, in fact anyone. If you are forced to, threaten to sue the airline.

4. Pretend to feel ill by dribbling diced carrots and milk down your chin. You will soon have plenty more room.

5. Set up your own airline that caters only for passengers you like.

☐ Tick here when you have spotted the Plan Pain

*RATE THE **PLANE PAIN'S** ANNOYANCE*

The Pollster

It is quite scary to think about how much information other people have about us. We bumble along through life believing that we are keeping ourselves to ourselves, when in fact there are companies and government officials out there collecting vast amounts of information about what we do, what we like, what we dislike and what we buy. Companies base their entire marketing strategies on the information they gather from our spending habits and from those terrible people that block your way in the high street – the Pollsters. Pollsters are used to gauge our opinions on all manner of things, from what we think about the current government to what types of products we use in our kitchens. It is through the Pollster that we get such statistics as 15 per cent of men between the ages of 30 and 60 want to spend more time with single naked women, or 90 per cent of 21 year olds believe they will never be able to retire. Most of the statistics churned out by these surveys are of course fixed and the information collected is only designed to feed into some alarmist newspaper article that provides free advertising. So the likely sponsors of the two statistics above could be an escort agency for the first one and a pension provider for the second.

Pollsters are often nosey middle-aged women with nothing better to do. They will stand in the centre of the pavement, clipboard in hand, looking the passers-by up and down to see if any of them fit the profile of the person they need to survey. If they do they will start with the "Excuse me, have you got five minutes to complete a survey?" routine. Having been snared on a few occasions I can safely say that most of the questions are designed in one way or another to reinforce a product or service. It soon becomes clear that the questions you are being asked are leading you down to a killer question, something like "Would you like to sign up for this fantastic credit card deal?"

As people have cottoned onto the Pollster, organisations have adopted other means to find out what we think about specific issues. So you can expect to see other types of Pollsters, such as the Focus Group, the Mystery Shopper, the Post Survey and the Beauty Babe. The first variant is at least more financially appealing than standing around in the high street. Here you are invited to participate in a staged discussion around a specific topic for which you are usually rewarded with some cash. You can get involved with all sorts of market research from what people might think about IT magazines (shite in the main, I'm sure) to road safety campaigns where you are invited to view pictures of car crashes and say which ones have the most impact. You also have the Mystery Shopper, which is another fun variant on the Pollster. Mystery Shoppers are paid to pop into shops and score the staff on the quality of service, the freshness of the food and other things like the general look and feel of the place. If they hate the staff they can give them a complete slating, which may end up with them getting a drubbing. Great. The Postal Survey usually comes under the guise of a lifestyle questionnaire. There are pages and pages of crazy questions that are designed to pry into almost every dimension of your life, from pets to sex. All of them offer some crap incentive like a free pencil or money off voucher for something you'd never want to buy. As you work through the questions it soon becomes apparent that the purpose of the survey is to fool you into answering yes to questions like "Will you be changing your car in the next year?" so that a Pushy Salesman or Cold Caller can use your answer to invade your privacy. Clearly people who answer these surveys are stupid. The final type is the Beauty Babe. This new type of Pollster is really a Pushy Salesman in disguise. Normally an attractive young woman, they will target middle-aged ladies and ask them questions about their skins, complexions, hair and other female-centric things. The whole point is to lead the discussion to the point where they can attempt to sell a wide variety of beauty products designed to make their punter look dazzling. In the final analysis the Pollster is the arch nosey parker who loves to get under your skin. Like so many things in public life, if we wanted to get involved or have our opinion aired we would seek to do it under our own steam.

ANNOYANCE RATING

2 - Compared to many of the pains you see the Pollster is not especially annoying. Sure, they block the pavement, clog up shopping centres and ask you inane questions, but they are a damn sight less intrusive than the plain Chugger variant of the Charity Chugger. The Pollsters who run focus groups are even less annoying because you are at the very least getting paid to give an opinion. The most annoying are the Pollsters who are trying to sell you something which, as always, is never what you want.

RARITY

3 – Pollsters do seem to be pretty rare. I have only been nabbed half a dozen times in my life and I don't see many of them around the towns and cities of the country. I also think there are fewer of them these days which may be explained by the increasing use of electronic means to capture the information companies need to segment the market.

SEASONAL VARIATIONS

None as such; Pollsters are primarily driven by the needs of their corporate masters rather than any season. This makes it difficult to predict when you are likely to spot them. The political Pollster will come out at election time and you will only tend to see the focus group organiser by invitation.

AVOIDANCE/REVENGE STRATEGIES

1. Take the opportunity to impart your personal opinion about the topic being addressed… it's vital to be heard.

2. Ignore the Pollster and walk past.

3. Stop and answer all the questions in Esperanto.

4. Design a survey yourself and make it extremely personal by asking questions about sexual and toilet habits – then target the Pollsters.

5. Fill in a postal survey on behalf of someone you dislike and answer yes to every question that is trying to sell something. Before long they will be inundated with Pushy Salesmen.

☐ Tick here when you have spotted the Pollster

RATE THE
POLLSTER'S
ANNOYANCE

The Protestor

We are fortunate to live in a democracy where, assuming you keep your nose clean, you won't be thrown in jail for complaining about what's wrong with the country. In many other nations across the world the opposite is true; if you so much as suggest that the ruling hierarchy sucks you are likely to disappear, never to be seen again. With the freedom of speech that we enjoy, it is important to use it when the opportunity arises, and what better way to do this than through protesting? There are many ways we can protest. We can write a letter to a newspaper, we can contact our local or national politician and we can phone in to television and radio shows. We can even make a statement by sewing up our mouths, doing a dirty protest or sitting on a pile of horse manure. Protestors are people who take this right to complain to the extreme. They will do their utmost not only to make a statement, but also to cause as much disruption as they can. Recently we heard of a bloke dressed as Spiderman running up a bill of £50 million as he spent almost two weeks perched on top of a crane. The police operation alone cost £10,000 a day and the disruption to businesses ran into the tens of millions. Then we have the regular anarchist and anti-capitalist days out, which are just an excuse to run amok in a large city, trash shops and businesses and steal as many hamburgers as possible from McDonalds. The Protestors will complain just about anything, but their main bugbears are the following:

- Road building, where they will dig tunnels under the proposed road, hide out in trees and live rough until they are physically removed from the site, die or get bored and go home for a bath.

- War: especially major conflicts overseas, such as Vietnam, The Gulf War, Iraq, Afghanistan and so on. In these instances Protestors will descend on London and other major cities across the world to march, complain about global domination and make peaceful overtones whilst often beating the shit out of the police.
- Student issues, which usually revolve around things like grants and tuition fees.
- Pay, which is a bit of a public sector sort of thing. In the private sector you can complain about your pay all you like, but you won't get any more money. Plus, you are more likely to be sacked or forced to leave.
- State pensions, which is when the Silver Protestor can be seen in force walking at a snail's pace using motorised wheelchairs, Zimmer frames and other devices that will keep them up long enough to complete the protest.

In the main Protestors are smelly, dirty, have nothing better to do and somehow believe they can make a difference. They sport dreadlocks and will play the samba as they dance down the street chanting their anti-capitalist and anti-establishment slogans. I muse to myself, as I watch them float by, that in about ten years – when many of them will have entered the economy on a more formal basis – they will become staunch, suit-wearing right-wingers complaining about unkempt youths protesting about some non-issue. I have witnessed this with many people, who used to dye their hair red, wear outlandish clothes and protest about nuclear arms. Most are now holding down six-figure-income jobs and bitching about trendy lefties holding the nation to ransom. Just look at the likes of Charles Clarke. He used to be head of the Student Union, defending the rights of his fellow students; now he sits in government ruining the education system for everyone and ensuring the next generation of students graduate into a sea of debt. It may seem trendy and fun living off the land and trying to overthrow the system when you're in your very late teens or early twenties, but you look a bit of an arse doing it in your forties.

ANNOYANCE RATING

7 – If you are trying to carry on with your normal life, the Protestor is very annoying. Most of us have resigned ourselves to just getting on with our lives and muttering under our breath about how bad things are. The braver ones amongst us will emigrate to get away from it all. The flipside is that we should cut the Protestors some slack, as some of the things they protest about are important and the only way things will change is if people rise up and crush the evil government repressing us. No, on second thoughts, it's all a waste of time.

RARITY

3 – Luckily, there are relatively few protests when we consider them in the round. Those that do occur tend to be short lived and after a while people just get bored of marching about the latest issue. Even the May Day Protestors are getting cheesed off with it all. Apparently, the anarchists and anti-capitalists can't agree what to do and they are all growing up anyway. Plus we shouldn't forget the aging of the population, which means most people will be too infirm to protest about anything, except perhaps the price of prescription drugs and hospital waiting lists.

SEASONAL VARIATIONS

None. Protestors are largely governed by what's happening in the country, the world and occasionally in their own streets. You will see them come out in force when a major geopolitical event is going down, or when an evil chancellor has yet again raised excise duty on a primary commodity. There are some Protestors who are more seasonal in their behaviour. Take the anarchists and anti-capitalists for example; they will turn up and march every May Day and every time there is an economic summit.

AVOIDANCE/REVENGE STRATEGIES

1. Never go out when a protest is on.

2. Produce a Protestor calendar, highlighting when major protests are going to occur. Why not include some pretty photographs of rioters clashing with police?

3. Start a protest about some innocuous issue, generate lots of interest and soon you will be at the head of a few hundred people shouting through loudhailers and blocking up the roads.

4. Interview Protestors and quiz them about why they haven't got proper jobs.

5. Join the police, dress up in riot gear and charge at them with nightsticks.

☐ Tick here when you have spotted the Protestor

RATE THE **PROTESTOR'S** *ANNOYANCE*

The Public Polluter

We have already come across the Dogmess Merchant. Now it is time to introduce one of their closest friends, the Public Polluter. Like the Dogmess Merchant, Public Polluters do not believe in following any acceptable norms of behaviour. As far as they are concerned, it is their god-given right to pollute the environment. The principal Public Polluters to watch out for include:

- The **Litter Louts**, who feel that the only place to discard their rubbish is anywhere but a dustbin, from irresponsible car drivers chucking out cans, papers, fags and the odd child to the hard-core louts who discard their unwanted cars on the roadside or in a local river. Then you have the Trolley Tippers, who leave shopping trolleys in car parks, local footpaths and woods. The Litter Lout is everywhere, from every village to every hilltop; even Everest is covered in the litter from all those heroic climbers attempting to reach the summit. It's a shame their mothers never taught them to tidy up after themselves.
- The **Chewing Gum Gits**, who insist on discarding their gum on the pavement – you thought those black marks were intentional? Some 20 million people consume more than 935 million packs of chewing gum each year and most just spit them out onto the pavement. Perhaps they would like me to vomit into their car air intakes in return? Apparently there are, on average, 20 pieces of gum on every square metre of pavement. That's a lot of gobbing. Local councils are introducing gum boards with faces of well-known, and probably hated, personalities on which the Chewing Gum Gits can posit their depleted boluses. This is a lot cheaper than the £20,000 they typically spend on cleaning it up each year.
- The **Fast Food Foulers**, who leave the remains of their burgers, kebabs, fish and chips and pizzas wherever they happened to finish them. Walking along the street the next

morning involves wading through fast food detritus, such as cabbage, half-eaten kebab, squashed burgers and the colourful packaging that goes with it.

- The **Pavement Pizzerias** often follow closely behind the Fast Food Foulers. They are the people who thought it was a great idea to mix booze and junk food but soon realised it was a grave mistake. I was told about a group of students on a field trip to Edinburgh who, having spent the whole day on the pop, decided to fill their bellies with pizzas. On the way home most of them were sick, many over the windows of the bus and most of them on the pavement. Few turned up for lectures the following morning. You can often see where the Pavement Pizzeria has walked by following the trail of mini pizzas along the street...

- The **Fag-End Throwers** who, on finishing their cigarette, will let the butt drift gracefully to the floor before stamping it out. Fortunately some authorities are getting tough on our yellow-fingered friends as one woman found out when she was fined £50 for dropping her fag end on the ground. Then of course there are the car park offenders, who choose to empty a year's worth of cigarette ends onto the floor of a multi-storey before driving off only to return to the exact same spot a year later to repeat the exercise – they clearly have a lot in common with salmon.

- The **Urinating Orang-utans** like to empty their bladders in public after consuming vast quantities of beer and spirits. If London is anything to go by, there are plenty of them around as some two million pints of urine are released onto the streets of London every year. I have witnessed the habit in broad daylight sometimes – not a pretty sight, as you observe a stream of yellow running down the pavement towards you. On a cold winter's night the Urinating Orang-utan can be easily spotted from the steam that surrounds him (they are usually male) as he empties his bladder. I even knew a Frenchman who had a preference for urinating on people's gardens over using public toilets. I can only assume this was because the general state of many public lavatories in France left a lot to be desired. And there is nothing like the caustic smell of urine to wake you up in the morning as you walk to the office. Urinating Orang-utans also make a bad job of using public toilets because they are so used to peeing on the ground that they seem incapable of containing the flow within the porcelain provided.

ANNOYANCE RATING

9 – Public Polluters are annoying for many reasons, not least for their fragrant abuse of common decency but principally for their tardy attitude to disposing of their waste. What I cannot understand is why they can't hold onto their trash, bladders and bowels until they get home. It seems they would rather dump their rubbish anywhere else and as a consequence ruin the look of every town, village and open space in the country.

RARITY
9 – The Public Polluter is everywhere. No matter where you turn you see the products of their bad manners. With new laws designed to persecute them, we may see a decline in their numbers. Plus, and assuming old people don't pollute the environment as much as the younger members of society, the aging population should stem the tide of litter, urine, chewing gum and other trash.

SEASONAL VARIATIONS
Public Polluters are certainly more prevalent during the **spring** and **summe**r when they are more likely to be out and about, having a quick slash, vomiting and discarding as much litter as they can. Winter tends to force them indoors where they probably belong.

AVOIDANCE|REVENGE STRATEGIES
1. Always hang out with clean, well-mannered and properly brought up people... you may not have many friends as a result, but at least you won't have urine-splattered shoes.

2. Dress up as a Womble and follow the Public Polluters wherever they go.

3. Ask your friendly dustmen to empty the contents of their dustcart into the Public Polluter's garden.

4. Stop them in the street and lecture them on how they are contributing to the burgeoning rat population, now in the region of 60 million.

5. Seek a change in legislation that brings in capital punishment for dropping any kind of litter. Judge Dredd would be very proud of you.

☐ Tick here when you have spotted the Public Polluter

RATE THE
PUBLIC POLLUTER'S
ANNOYANCE

The Pushy Salesman

GENERAL CHARACTERISTICS

Selling, whether oneself or a specific product, is a skill that many of us have to develop throughout our working lives. When we look at the spectrum of salespeople, we can observe two extreme types. At one end we have the silver-tongued salesman who plies his art with skill, panache and plenty of grease, whilst at the other, we have the rank amateur, who is generally rubbish at selling and prefers to coerce rather than persuade the punters. These are the Pushy Salesmen who pester, cajole and bully us until we capitulate. They can, of course, be female as well as male, and no matter where we turn we find them…

- In shopping centres where we are attacked by the mobile phone salesmen, hovering a few yards away from their shop fronts. Very often they are overweight, intellectually challenged spotty youths who have clearly failed to apply themselves at school. They stand uncomfortably, swaying from side to side mentally rehearsing their pathetic sales pitch and will accost you as you walk past asking "Do you want a free mobile phone?" If I wanted a phone, which I don't, I would have asked. My son, who is 12, was recently approached by one of these youths and on being asked the standard "Do you want a free mobile?" responded with "No, I would rather die!" That's my boy.

- In shops themselves, when you are happily browsing, they will come up to you and see if you need any help. They are probably taught that this is the best way to make their customers feel loved and wanted, when in fact all we want is to be left alone. What's more, this normally acts as a deterrent to getting customers through the door, especially if the store happens to be empty. Maybe there's a correlation?

- In the home, where you will have to contend with the pushy insurance and double glazing salesmen. Inviting them into your home in the first place is bad enough but getting them out is almost impossible. Insurance salesmen will draw graphs, foam at the mouth and tell you how much money you will make. Of course, most of the stuff they peddle is snake oil and normally involves you losing your shirt. The double glazing salesmen are more expert at making you feel bad if you don't buy.

I heard one story that involved a couple being lectured to by a pushy vacuum cleaner salesman. The guy was sufficiently forward to get an appointment and when he arrived it turned out that he was attempting to flog what looked like an early 1920s Hoover. He spent over two hours showing how great it was at removing dust, water, baby's vomit and all manner of things from the floor. By the end of the extensive display, the salesman had virtually cleaned the couple's house. Then came the sting in the tail: the machine cost £1,600! For a bloody vacuum cleaner? The couple, of course, balked at the cost, at which point the salesman got very aggressive; he only left after a heated row, and without a sale. You can find the Pushy Salesman anywhere in the world. A number of years ago I was in Kenya with a friend and we were walking along one of the main streets in Nairobi. A man popped out from nowhere and asked if we wanted to buy some postcards. "No thanks," we replied but "no" was clearly not in his vocabulary. He continued to follow us down the street repeating his "Do you want some postcards?" mantra. Our ability to remain polite was tested to breaking point and a few hundred yards further, we both turned around and shouted "Why don't you just f#@/* off!", which he duly did. The fundamental problem with Pushy Salesmen is that they fail to understand that if I (or indeed anyone) actually wanted to buy something, we would ask. We don't need some idiot foisting unwanted products and services on us.

ANNOYANCE RATING

9 – Pushy Salesmen are annoying because they are like the Terminator; they won't stop until they have sold you something, even if you don't want it. Whether it's insurance, double glazing, cars or mobile phones they are all the same. Push, push, push. Perhaps if they were not so pushy, they might be more successful. The most annoying Pushy Salesmen are – of course – Estate Agents who like to think they are at the leading edge of sales techniques, when if fact they are wide boys (and girls) acting as unsophisticated middlemen.

RARITY

8 – In my opinion there are just too many Pushy Salesmen around. Maybe we should cull them from time to time?

SEASONAL VARIATIONS

The Pushy Salesman is mainly driven by quarterly sales targets, so you will experience increased pushiness towards the end of **March, June, September** and **December**. Mind you, this is often the best time to get a good deal... every cloud has a silver lining.

AVOIDANCE/REVENGE STRATEGIES

1. Beware anyone with scuffed shoes and an ill-fitting or double-breasted suit who comes up to you with a cheesy smile.

2. Pretend to be an overseas visitor and have wandered into the store thinking it was the train station.

3. When replying to the Pushy Salesman, why not spit at the same time so that you can cover their face in phlegm?

4. Wear dark glasses and plug up your ears with cotton wool so that you can browse in peace.

5. Wear a T-shirt that says "I club pushy salespeople to death".

☐ Tick here when you have spotted the Pushy Salesman

RATE THE
**PUSHY
SALESMAN'S**
ANNOYANCE

The Queue Jumper

GENERAL CHARACTERISTICS

There is something peculiarly British when it comes to queues and queuing. We will stand in line, sometimes quite literally for hours, queuing up for something. We wait patiently, keeping ourselves to ourselves and shuffling along slowly until we are at the front. Now, if we can adhere to the basic principals and etiquette of queuing then it is reasonable to expect that others should do the same. Unfortunately there are those who don't. These are the Queue Jumpers. The Queue Jumper is someone who believes that those who queue must be stupid because when you can push in, why bother waiting at the back? Overseas visitors are especially prone to pushing into the front of the line, which really makes the diligent queuer's blood boil. Now before you start on some xenophobic rant about bloody foreigners coming over here and forcing themselves into the front of the ice cream queue, I would just like to provide an explanation as to why. There is a dimension to national culture called uncertainty avoidance (for those interested, look up the work of Geert Hofstede), which refers to a nationality's ability to cope with situations that involve uncertainty. In those countries with high uncertainty avoidance people cannot cope with not knowing whether there will be any ice cream left by the time they get to the front of the queue. So in order to create the certainty that they will get a ninety-nine with a flake they will push in. The opposite is true for those, such as the British, who have a low uncertainty avoidance. We are pretty certain there will be an ice cream for us when we reach the window and, in any case, if there isn't any left we'll just forget about it and go elsewhere. This inability to cope with queuing also helps to explain why certain nationalities insist on placing their towels on the sun loungers by the swimming pool. It seems that even we British are getting less willing to hang around in line. Some recent

research identified our increasing reluctance to wait in queues and also the growing incidence of queue rage, when people, quite rightly in my mind, get violent when other people try to push in. Apparently old people love hanging around in queues because it gives them the opportunity to discuss the war, the Queen Mother and the state of the old age pension. Couples often end up arguing and then walk off continuing their heated debate about wasting time standing in line. Young people and overseas visitors just push in.

The Queue Jumpers ply their trade in all manner of circumstances. At theme parks they will wind their way through the often unending queue of adolescents claiming to be trying to find their relatives. They ignore the complaints and comments from the queue-abiding citizens waiting their turn. At ice cream vans they will walk straight to the front without any consideration for those behind them. At supermarkets they will muscle their way between you and the till thinking that just because they are old or just plain stupid they have the right to pop their goods on the conveyor belt before you. Thankfully many establishments are beginning to support queuing by introducing more effective queuing systems. Theme parks will eject Queue Jumpers, and there are even lessons on queuing for overseas visitors and posters warning them of the consequences of queue jumping. Queue Jumpers represent the worst in society. They are ignorant, insensitive and ought to be despatched to a desert island and left to rot. There are always exceptions to any rule, of course. I was running very late for a flight having spent ages trying to find somewhere to park. As I dashed into the terminal building I heard "Would Mr Holmes please proceed to Gate 5 immediately, where the flight is ready to depart." Running to the check-in queue I saw an incredibly long line of disgruntled passengers (of course). I knew I didn't have enough time, so I went straight to the front and asked to be checked in, explaining that my name had been called over the Tannoy. Although the check-in staff were very accommodating, everyone behind me made comments, looked thoroughly hacked off and shot me looks that would have turned the Medusa to stone. After a mad dash to the departure gate, I managed to make the flight.

ANNOYANCE RATING

7 – Queue Jumpers are very annoying. Why should they be given service before you, when you have been waiting patiently for your turn? The annoyance rating shoots off the dial when the person behind the counter actually serves the Queue Jumper first. Uproar often ensues as people shout and spit blood.

RARITY

3 – In general the British are pretty good at observing queue etiquette, which means that, apart from the odd exception, there are relatively few Queue Jumpers around. However, if we include overseas visitors, especially those from Europe, then the number of people pushing in increases sharply.

SEASONAL VARIATIONS

Summer will always bring out far more Queue Jumpers than winter. This is because there is more to queue for: ice creams, tombola stalls, theme park rides and museums. The most extreme form of queue jumping can be found during the **January sales**, particularly at places like Harrods. People will camp out overnight in order to be at the front of the queue when the sale starts. When the doors open they will run with everyone else to secure the best deals. The problem is that when they get to the tills there is a sea of people shouting, pushing and generally ignoring the need to queue. They might as well steal the goods, because no one is paying attention.

AVOIDANCE|REVENGE STRATEGIES

1. Avoid all queues by only going to places outside peak time.

2. Chill out; in the end we'll all get served and at least you won't suffer from a heart attack because some spotty oik has got a hot dog before you.

3. As they walk past having queue jumped and got their goods before you, trip the Queue Jumpers up so that they drop their purchases all over the floor.

4. Design an elaborate queuing system complete with barriers, CCTV and information notices. Better still, make sure the corridor in which the people queue can only just fit one person by lining it with razor wire.

5. Patrol queues with a cattle prod and give those who attempt to push in a little reminder of queue etiquette.

☐ Tick here when you have spotted the Queue Jumper

RATE THE
QUEUE JUMPER'S
ANNOYANCE

The Raging Bull

GENERAL CHARACTERISTICS

The nature and complexity of modern life creates an environment in which many people feel they have lost control of their lives. They really can't cope with the stresses and strains caused by the transport system (as we have seen with the Belligerent in *Pains on Trains*), work (see the Stress Junkie in *Pains in the Office*), looking after elderly parents and young children and having to deal with incompetent banks, building societies, local government officials, and so on and so on. When faced with a stressful situation the brain sets up one of two responses: fight or flight. Although it might be preferable to opt for the second outcome, our primitive brain usually overrides our frontal lobes so the former behaviour tends to dominate. People who cannot control this basic instinct are known as Raging Bulls. The Raging Bull has given rise to a wide range of phenomena, including:

- Road Rage. Apparently Road Rage can happen to anybody at anytime and can range from the odd expletive or two to physical violence and even murder. With high levels of congestion, non-stop roadworks and incompetent drivers, Road Rage is increasingly common. Typical of the Road Rager is driving on the horn. No matter what is happening in front of them they will be banging their fists on the horn and waving them at each driver they meet. If they are not using the horn, they will be flashing their headlights. They also love sitting on your tail and driving less than three feet from your rear bumper.
- Church Rage. Of all the places you should least expect to see the Raging Bull the church is one. Think again. There have been numerous cases of churchgoers hurling

ecclesiastical abuse at many a poor reverend. In one case an archbishop was accosted by a bunch of finger-jabbing women who accused him of destroying the Catholic Church, saying he (personally, presumably) was responsible for abortion and homosexuality. With stories like these, I reckon everyone will be flooding back to church to pick up a piece of the action.

- Car Park Rage. You can understand this one, I I guess, especially when there are more cars than car parking spaces. Having travelled a long distance to get somewhere only to find there are no parking spaces is a very stressful experience. Tempers fray and arguments flare as motorists exchange expletives over the last parking space. A body builder was recently charged with assault when he beat up a 70-year-old gentleman whom he believed had taken his space. In another incident, an elderly lady's tyres were slashed after she had "stolen" a slot from a waiting car. Car parks are increasingly coming to resemble war zones.

- Supermarket Rage. The Supermarket, as we will see with the Supermarket Sadist, is a fertile ground for the Raging Bull. In one incident a woman attacked a fellow shopper who had more items than were permitted for the "12 items only" queue. The female shopper, who only had thirteen items, was standing in the queue when the Raging Bull behind her piped up with "Some people just don't know how to count". The woman turned round and said, "Do you have a problem with me?" "Yes," came the reply, followed by a tirade of abuse. The Raging Bull then followed the woman out of the supermarket and down the street. Eventually the woman who was being followed turned and said, "Could you just leave me alone?" at which point the Raging Bull laid into her, pulled her hair, kneed her in the stomach and kicked her in the head. All over a small packet of custard creams… some people.

The Raging Bull is typical of the person who prefers to settle their differences through violent means. In one incident Tony Blair was attacked with powder bombs in the House of Commons. The protest by Fathers 4 Justice smacked of the Gunpowder Plot, but without the gunpowder, the Catholics or the consequences… shame.

ANNOYANCE RATING

6 – As long as you are not having to deal with them, the Raging Bull can offer wonderful entertainment. I love the way they get so worked up over such trivial things. I'd like to see them in a really stressful situation; I suspect they would have a seizure. Naturally, if you happen to be on the receiving end of the Raging Bull it is likely to be a scary experience.

RARITY

6 - The number of angry people is on the increase. People are becoming less and less tolerant of their fellow human beings and rather than discuss things in a sensible way, there is a tendency to resort to verbal abuse and physical violence. Road Rage, in particular, is becoming very common and it is that which has spawned the other types of rage incidents. It won't be long before we have WI Rage with the ladies at the Women's Institute exchanging blows over who is running the cake stall.

SEASONAL VARIATIONS

Driven by the weather. It is well known that as the ambient temperature rises, our tempers shorten. When it gets to anything above 80 degrees Fahrenheit our ability to control our rage reduces dramatically. So in other words, you should expect to see a lot more of the Raging Bull when it is **hot and sunny**. The other time of year when you can spot more Raging Bulls is **Christmas** and the **sales season**. Here you will see more car parking incidents and other forms of shopping rage.

AVOIDANCE/REVENGE STRATEGIES

1. Give the Raging Bull a copy of the *Little Book of Calm*. Sit down with them, cross-legged, and chant some of the entries together. Why not burn some incense at the same time?

2. Learn ju-jitsu and break the Raging Bull's legs when you are attacked.

3. Arm yourself with a samurai sword.

4. Keep a tranquillizer gun about your person. Ideally the darts should be strong enough to floor an elephant.

5. Set up an anger management course that involves a group of people shouting and abusing the Raging Bull. At the end of this, he or she will be a retiring wallflower.

☐ Tick here when you have spotted the Raging Bull

RATE THE
RAGING BULL'S
ANNOYANCE

The Religious Nut

eligion is, I think, a very personal affair. What you believe is something that you need to reconcile with yourself and, of course, your maker – should you ever meet him or her. No matter what you hold to be true I also think it is important to keep your feelings to yourself unless invited to give an opinion. As they say, the two things you should always avoid at dinner parties are politics and religion. Despite millions of people worshipping their god in a private and personal way, there is a significant minority who feel obliged to ram their beliefs down your throat. Such people are called Religious Nuts. The Religious Nuts are known for their obsession with the religion of their choice. Not content with walking around with that "I'm alright, Jack" look about them, they will insist on telling you that unless you adopt their beliefs you will be eternally damned. Hmm; I always thought that religious people were there to convince you of the merits of joining their happy throng, rather than issuing you with an ultimatum. You see, that's the fundamental problem with the Religious Nuts; they fail to see any point of view other than the one that has been imparted to them by their particular religious leader. Not only that, but they can be some of the nastiest, most vindictive people you can ever hope to meet.

My wife used to work with a Religious Nut in one of the high street banks. The chap concerned was not particularly great at his job and, if we are being brutally honest, had little if any prospects of progressing beyond his somewhat lowly grade. He would tell my wife and her colleagues that unless they repented of their sins and believed in his god they would be eternally damned. I was told one story that involved a student who was spending some time with an old school friend whom he hadn't seen for quite a few years. It was great to meet up again and reminisce about how much fun they had when they

were at school; all those wild parties, all that booze, all that vomit! Then, on the Sunday, the friend asked the student if would like to come to a church service. Not wanting to offend and being mildly religious himself, the student decided to go. Anyway, everything was going swimmingly until the pastor asked if anyone had performed a miracle that week. A few hands shot up and then he asked that everyone should speak in tongues (now this is something that the Religious Nuts are particularly skilled at, as it sets them aside from the average churchgoer). Immediately a couple of hundred hands shot up and those people all proceeded to speak gobbledegook, cry, scream and, by the look of it, wet their pants. The poor student didn't know where to put himself and merely sunk his head into his hands until it was time to go. He never saw his friend again.

You often see groups of Religious Nuts (I guess you have to call them flocks) in town centres. They will congregate on a Saturday afternoon and stand in a circle or semi-circle taking it in turns to read great chunks of text from the Bible. Then, when exhausted, they hand the baton onto the next person. They do this for hours on end and only bugger off when the shopping centre closes. What is especially amusing about the whole affair is the way the general public shoots them amazed looks whilst giving them the widest berth possible. If you hit the big time in Religious Nut circles you can become a celebrity, which normally means you can enter the religious equivalent of the lecture circuit. This can involve inviting thousands of gullible people into a vast auditorium where they will part with loads of cash to hear a preacher talk bollocks for a couple of hours and perform the odd miracle. And, if you really hit it big, you can have your own TV show, which is very American. From time to time, the Religious Celebs will show their true colours by being convicted of fraud, embezzlement, sleeping with prostitutes and a whole host of other often illegal activities which they had been warning their flocks about. Despite such obvious shows of human fallibility the Religious Nuts will do anything they can to hang onto the belief that there is more to life than a shit job, crap neighbours, loveless marriage and halitosis.

ANNOYANCE RATING

5 – Religious Nuts drive the non-religious amongst the population mad. Why must they ram it down our throats? Maybe they would like other people to push their beliefs and convictions on them… you know, like the Dogger, perhaps. But I guess they will respond with the usual "you're going to hell" routine and look smug. Well, let's see who's smug when they turn to dust like the rest of us. Of course, we'll never know…

RARITY

8 – We are inundated with Religious Nuts. They are all around us, like the cast of the Body Snatchers. I am also sure that as people get older and realise that they are not as immortal as they once thought, they turn to religion in desperation, hoping that there is more to life than this mortal coil.

SEASONAL VARIATIONS

Predictably, you will see much more of the Religious Nuts at **key religious events** such as Passover, Christmas, Easter and whenever their chosen religion states is a key time. Traditionally you will also see plenty just before a millennium when they fear that the end of the world is nigh. We saw (although I wasn't there) lots of them around 1000 AD and we saw another bunch more recently. In extreme cases Religious Nuts will shut themselves away in a cave or building somewhere and then top themselves in the hope that they will be treated well on judgement day. All that's left is a pile of bodies for the authorities to clear up, which is mighty inconsiderate.

AVOIDANCE/REVENGE STRATEGIES

1. Be tolerant and interested in all religions.

2. Tell the Religious Nuts that you believe in whatever they do to get them off your back.

3. Give them a copy of Monty Python's *Life of Brian*.

4. Dress up as Beelzebub and harass them.

5. Set up a religious cult that involves foaming at the mouth, self-flagellation and listening to Abba.

☐ Tick here when you have spotted the Religious Nut

RATE THE
RELIGIOUS NUT'S
ANNOYANCE

The Restaurant Rat

What is it about restaurants that brings out the worst in people? They have become the hunting ground for the pretentious. So whilst the proletariat may pop into their local fast food joint for a pizza or burger and chips, the bourgeoisie must go to places where they have to pay through the nose. The Restaurant Rats are ostentatious ponces who love to inform their friends, colleagues and general acquaintances that they have been to some fancy joint run by a well-known chef. They will tell you how exquisite the meal was, how superb the wine tasted and how they complemented the celebrity chef on a job well done. Quite frankly, the chef could have served up a turd and they would have said how wonderful it was. Restaurant Rats will typically go to the expensive joints because this demonstrates to those around them that they are people who can afford the outlandish prices charged by such establishments. The other thing the Rat will do is to continue their flamboyant display with the wine. They will study the wine list in great detail, regaling the other guests with the quality of the grape and lineage of the vineyard. If they are especially flashy, they will let you know that they know the owner of the vineyard and how they can get hold of the wine at discounted prices. Having bored you witless with what they know about the wine, they will select a bottle (usually the cheapest) and, once it has been opened, will drape a napkin over their arm and swill the wine in the glass to test its quality. Not satisfied with this ridiculous display they will then instruct you on how you can tell how old the wine is from the shape of the diamond projected onto the napkin. And all you wanted was half a bottle of vino to deaden your senses so you could cope with being with such a crushing bore.

Restaurant Rats are everywhere. Not long ago there was an outburst from none other than Princess Michael of Kent who allegedly told a group of boisterous Americans to go back to the colonies. During the flare-up she banged on their table with her fists; such polite behaviour from someone in the highest echelon of society. More recently we have seen the unholy alliance of the Celeb, the Attention Seeker and the Restaurant Rat. The latest manifestation of the Reality TV phenomenon has conjured up a bunch of Celebs who, being desperate for attention, subjected themselves to fifteen days of being beaten up by a celebrity chef. Not satisfied with filling a couple of kitchens with a bunch of has-beens, the food was then served up to a room full of C-list Celebs who, equally in need of enhancing their otherwise dead careers, had to be seen posing for the cameras with the usual inane grins and giving their critical comments on the food cooked up by the desperate teams. Then you have the food critics from the press. Often grossly overweight and waiting patiently for their Type 2 diabetes to set in, they will cast their eyes over the food and come out with a load of pompous and conceited comments which are designed to show that they have something interesting to say about it. You see, that's the problem with the Restaurant Rats; they talk complete and utter bollocks about food. This need for flowery language has fuelled a linguistic revolution in catering. No longer satisfied with using plain language to describe a meal, it is now necessary for restaurant owners to apply the linguistic skills of a wizard to impress the punters and justify the ridiculous prices they charge. So instead of chips and gravy you are served up with pommes frites served on a bed of caramelised onion gravy with a soupçon of garlic and a suggestion of oregano. What's the difference? About ten pounds. The other thing this allows the restaurant to do is to serve incredibly small portions beautifully presented on the plate before you. After a three-course meal somewhere like this you have no alternative but to stop by your local kebab van on your way home to get something to sate your hunger.

ANNOYANCE RATING

7 – I actually like going to restaurants, but what I detest is the showy rubbish that is talked about them. People who talk such tosh are so boorish and are only doing it to make them look like pseudo-intellectuals. It's just a restaurant, for heaven's sake. Couple this with deliberately loud conversations, mobile phones and children who have no concept of table manners or what a knife and fork are for and you might as well stay at home.

RARITY

6 – As a nation we are eating out more and more and despite the dip in the number of investment bankers spending fortunes on their celebratory meals, the number of Restaurant Rats is increasing. I think that human nature is playing its part, particularly in relation to keeping up with, or ideally overtaking, the Joneses in the restaurant stakes and – I guess – in the obesity stakes too.

SEASONAL VARIATIONS

There are **few real seasonal variations** in the Restaurant Rat's behaviour. They are largely driven by economic cycle. When they are on their uppers they will be satisfied with chicken and chips, but when they are flush they will get onto the waiting list of the country's top establishments to both demonstrate that they are wealthy enough to have the funds for such extravagance and show they are better than the average punter.

AVOIDANCE|REVENGE STRATEGIES

1. Go to your local chippy; it's wholesome, good value and convenient.

2. Don't go to overpriced restaurants run by celebrity chefs.

3. Learn to cook yourself so you don't have to overspend on fancy nights out.

4. Go up to Restaurant Rats, pick up their plates of overpriced shite and pour it over their heads.

5. Cook the Restaurant Rat and serve on a bed of pillau rice with a red wine jus and a sprinkling of coconut shavings.

☐ Tick here when you have spotted the Restaurant Rat

RATE THE
**RESTAURANT
RAT'S**
ANNOYANCE

The School Runner

There has been a fundamental shift in the way we think about how we educate our children. For a long time most of us went to our local school irrespective of its reputation. It was a bit of a lottery; some schools had a great reputation, whilst others had a poor one. So apart from the toffee-nosed twats who sent their kids off to boarding school, the majority of us would make do with what we got. This also meant that most kids would walk to school. No longer restricted to their local schools, they now have this wonderful thing called parental choice, which means they can – at least in theory – have their offspring educated wherever they like. No longer restricted to crap schools with crap teachers they can try and get into the good schools with the best teachers. This normally means that the schools are much further away from home than in the past. Parents are also petrified that their progeny will be abducted by the many perverts that wander the streets or be run over by the myriad of nutcases on the roads. And many more parents work. This means that both mum and dad are in a tearing hurry in the morning to get the kids dressed, fed and packed off to school before they charge off themselves. No more gentle walks along leafy village streets; it's get in the car, put the pedal to the metal and drive like a loony to the school gates. Welcome to the School Runner. Twenty years ago one in three children walked on their own to school. Today this is one in nine. It should come as no surprise that the number of journeys to school by car has almost doubled to 30 per cent. At the start and end of the school day one in five cars on urban roads is ferrying one or more kids to and from their place of learning. This is helping to extend the average commuter's journey by 50 per cent. Parents are now getting so stressed out by the school run that they are posing an enormous risk to other road users. A recent investigation found

that the heartbeats of mothers driving their little darlings to school more than doubled, which apparently significantly impairs judgement whilst behind the wheel. Some 69 per cent regularly break the speed limit and 54 per cent jump red lights in order to get their children there on time. Not surprising, then, that around 25 per cent have been involved in accidents. The School Runner is characterised by:

- A complete disrespect for other road users, particularly pedestrians. For them it's a race against time. They cannot wait for school kids to cross the road even when there is a Lollipop Man present. In one village there was a standoff between the Lollipop Man who was diligently ferrying the children across the road and an irate father who was getting increasingly enraged at the delay. The more the father got annoyed, the more the Lollipop Man waited for the children. The driver was shouting out of his window, banging his horn and shaking his fist. After about ten minutes of this the Lollipop Man let him pass and received a stream of abuse.
- An inability to park in safe places. Many will park their cars by railings, in bus stops, lay-bys, on zebra crossings and on the pavement as they walk little Johnny the final five metres to the front entrance.
- An obsession with status. Yes, even the school run has become a status thing for the anxious middle classes. Trendy parents can't just bring their children to school in any old motor; it must be a new, top of the range, ideally gargantuan, 4x4. They must look better than the other School Runners. The size of these vehicles is ridiculous for the trip they are undertaking and only serves to make it impossible to get through, even with a Smart Car.

In the final analysis, School Runners are products of their own making. The combination of irrational fear, laziness, status consciousness and atrocious driving skills has made the journey to school a life-threatening affair. It's time the School Runners used their feet. Who knows, they might even get to know their children and may even lose some weight in the process.

ANNOYANCE RATING

8 – The School Runner is a menace and is responsible for many of the ills that beset today's society. They are partly responsible for the rise in obesity because they cannot be arsed to let their children walk a few hundred yards to school. They are single-handedly responsible for the increased congestion on our roads and they are almost certainly a factor in the increased number of car accidents involving school children.

RARITY

9 - With so few people walking to school these days, the School Runner is very common. Lazy parents can be seen ejecting their overweight brats in the same way a jumpmaster does on a charity parachute jump. If you listen carefully, you can hear "go, go, go!" as they are ejected from the 4x4.

SEASONAL VARIATIONS

Although you will see the School Runner throughout the year, they will obviously be restricted to **term times**. And, I can tell you, what bliss it is when it's half term… not a 4x4 in sight. The other thing you will notice is the deterioration in their driving skills during the **winter**. Then the School Runners will undoubtedly knock more kids over, crash their Range Rovers more often and make even more of a bloody nuisance of themselves than they do in the summer.

AVOIDANCE|REVENGE STRATEGIES

1. Always walk your children to school and if you can't do this make sure they use their bicycles or take the bus.

2. Let the School Runner's tyres down.

3. Get your local council to paint double yellow lines on all the roads within a three-mile radius of the school.

4. Steal a fire engine and drive it at speed through all the badly parked cars.

5. Import the largest, most lurid and most swanky Sports Utility Vehicle from the US and drive your kids to school in it. Try and park it in the most dangerous of places so that people cannot miss it.

☐ Tick here when you have spotted the School Runner

RATE THE
SCHOOL RUNNER'S
ANNOYANCE

The Smoker

moking began some five thousand years ago when the Egyptians burnt sweet herbs and frankincense whilst making sacrifices to their gods. During the early Christian period it was believed that inhaling the smoke from burning hare's fur and goat's horn cured illnesses like consumption. No one is quite sure how tobacco, which is what most people smoke today, was discovered. All we do know is that crude cigarettes were being smoked by the Mayans in Mexico and that dear old Christopher Columbus brought tobacco to Europe after his trip to the New World in 1492. Sir Walter Raleigh popularised smoking at Queen Elizabeth's court and was even having a final drag as the axe lopped off his head. But it is Casanova who has the claim to fame of being the first European to smoke cigarettes, which I guess he had to given how many lovers he had – dying of cancer may have seemed preferable to syphilis. The mass production of cigarettes began in 1853 and the industry hasn't looked back since. Despite this illustrious and fascinating history, the Smoker is a modern-day pariah. This is the Smoker's second appearance in the Pains trilogy, as we have already seen them in the guise of Chimneystacks in *Pains in the Office*. I'm not apologising; I hate Smokers and I am not alone. Anti-smoking is nothing new, as Pope Urban VIII banned it in the churches of Seville and there was an anti-smoking lobby as far back as 1648. There are numerous reasons why the Smoker is detested so, and why they earn a place in this book as well. First, they stink out public places, like bars, cafés, restaurants, parks, beaches, shopping centres and anywhere where people congregate. Second, they often smell. Third, they litter the streets with fag ends. And, finally, they waste valuable hospital beds. Walking along the street dodging the clouds of blue smoke that are emitted by the Smokers is bad enough, but going into a pub for a pint is a tear-inducing,

gut-wrenching experience. The same thing happens in restaurants. You settle down for a nice meal that you ought to be able to savour and then you find you are sitting next to the smoking section. This really, really upsets non-smokers because their meal is ruined by the wafts of exhaled tobacco drifting over to them as they are eating. What I can't understand is how the smoking diners manage to fit in at least four cigarettes during a two-course meal. I am sure they can't taste a thing. The other thing about Smokers is that when out with friends they never bother to ask if those around them mind if they light up. They'll set fire to their tobacco and puff their smoke into the faces of those around them without a care in the world. And who was it that said manners maketh man? The Smoker is now being attacked from all sides. The most bizarre example was of a guy who killed his wife after she smoked more than her daily allowance of six cigarettes; apparently she was supposed to be giving up. On the other hand, one New York smoker attacked someone who asked him to put out his cigarette and stabbed him to death. But probably the strangest thing with smoking is that there are porn websites dedicated to those who want to watch couples having sex while smoking. I guess it gives a whole new meaning to the words blow job...

The default state of any Smoker is one of intense irritation until they can have their next fag, so it's no wonder that they are up in arms against the increasing pressure for them to give up or smoke in the most inconvenient of places. As a student, I used to smoke the odd cigar or two, especially when watching Clint Eastwood films. A friend and myself went to see *Pale Rider* and took a packet of cigars with us into the cinema. Throughout the film we would light up and puff away pretending to be Clint and repeating the lines from the film: yes, I know, Movie-Going Morons... We found this intensely amusing and, having enjoyed the film, decided to hang back and watch it a second time. After all, we had to finish the packet of cigars. Anyway, we were settling back lighting up for the fifth time, when the usher came up to us and reminded us that it was a non-smoking cinema. We were suitably embarrassed.

ANNOYANCE RATING

10 – Speaking as a non-smoker, then I can happily say that the Smoker scores ten out of ten for annoyance. There is nothing quite as bad as coming home from a night out, or a brief trip to the pub, stinking of smoke. Smokers, of course, disagree.

RARITY

7 – Although a few Smokers are listening to the health warnings and giving up, some 30 per cent of the population continues with this filthy habit. Taken globally, there are now around 1.3 billion smokers in the world, which is expected to rise to 2.2 billion by 2050. So, I don't think we'll be seeing less of our wheezing friends for some time to come. The only consolation is that the number of Smokers killing themselves will rise from 4.2 million every year to 8.4 million.

SEASONAL VARIATIONS

None, the Smoker will be filling our lungs with secondary smoke all year round.

AVOIDANCE/REVENGE STRATEGIES

1. Avoid anyone who smokes.

2. Spray rat poison around the Smoker and when confronted, just say you're doing it because you find it relaxing.

3. Follow the Smokers with a hose pipe and douse them in water every time they light up.

4. The next time you are in a restaurant, pose as a waiter and offer to sprinkle a cocktail of 4,000 toxic chemicals on their food. It's quicker and cheaper than lighting up.

5. Introduce draconian new laws that require all smokers to be locked up at home along with a cigarette machine. The money spent on buying their tabs can be used to pay for their hospital bills.

☐ Tick here when you have spotted the Smoker

RATE THE
SMOKER'S
ANNOYANCE

The Soap Obsessed

GENERAL CHARACTERISTICS

minent scientists and health gurus tell us that one of the principal reasons why the world is becoming obese is a lack of exercise. The launch of the stupid, nanny-state campaign in which the public is encouraged to walk for half an hour a day is doomed to failure. You see, the fundamental reason why our waistlines are getting bigger is because of our unwillingness to get our fat butts off the sofa and away from the television. Although many will claim that the television provides us with a wealth of educational programming, it is fair to say that most of it is chewing gum for the eyes, shite in other words. Apart from the current obsession for cheap reality TV programming, the worst offenders are the soap operas. The term "soap opera" dates back to the corporate sponsorship of radio shows. Over time soap companies dominated this sponsorship and rival manufacturers would fund the competing serialised melodramas. Most of these were targeted at the romance-starved American housewife who, of course, was a major purchaser of soap powder. Today soap operas dominate the small screen and, it seems, people's lives – and not just those of women, before male readers get smug. Such people I call the Soap Obsessed. You see, the Soap Obsessed is just that, obsessed; they are obsessed with the storylines, they are obsessed with the characters and they are particularly obsessed with social issues portrayed within their favourite programmes. For these people, the fictitious characters are actually real people, not actors following a script. They will talk about them as though they were their own flesh and blood. Take *Friends*, for example; the last episode of this show had something in the region of 85 million viewers, almost a third of the entire population of the US. One channel even cancelled its prime time programmes

in order to stream images of people watching it on their televisions. You could see people crying, laughing and looking dejected as the credits rolled for the very last time. They had finally come to terms with the fact that a major part of their life had been taken from them. One woman even wrote an article in the press in which she admitted she was booing throughout the final show and that she felt distraught, cheated, bereft, alone and that her life would never be the same again. How utterly sad is that? Apparently the same thing occurred when *Sex and the City* ended. Call me heartless, but what is up with these people and why do they become so completely wrapped up in these programmes? All I can offer up as an explanation is that it's a form of escapism which is less harmful than doing drugs. With such depressing storylines, I suspect that viewers feel good about themselves because their lives can never be as bad as those of the characters portrayed in the soap. There are many traits of the Soap Obsessed that are irritating. First, you are never allowed to disturb them whilst the show is on; no talking, no witty comments, no telephone calls, nothing. Soap time is sacred time. Second, they will spend hours discussing the storylines and whether Dirty Den is going knife Pete in the temple with his old scout knife, or Ken Barlow is going to have sex with Deirdre and a Shetland pony (although how he'd tell them apart nobody knows). These discussions are often heated and accompanied by a foaming at the mouth usually only seen in rabies victims. Third, and this is probably the worst part, they believe that the soaps are important conduits for social issues. They will tell you that because certain storylines focus on murder, rape, homosexuality, arson, teenage pregnancy, line dancing and so on, they are doing the nation a service. This somehow absolves them from the guilt that comes from wasting a vast proportion of their lives watching the television. In order to justify these storylines, the television programmers will provide helpline numbers for people who want to discuss the issues raised during the show. Not satisfied with watching the bloody programmes, the Soap Obsessed will buy magazines dedicated to their favourite soaps and soap stars. Such magazines will give them important insights into the characters' lives on and off the screen, will hint at future plots and be full of crappy images of the B-list stars congratulating themselves at the annual soap awards.

ANNOYANCE RATING

5 – This is very much a preference thing and probably falls right down the middle of the annoyance scale. There are certainly many people who love the soaps and will get on well with the Soap Obsessed, because they are Soap Obsessed too. Equally, and thankfully, there are a significant number of people who hate the soaps with a vengeance. They hate having to pussyfoot around the Soap Obsessed, and they get incredibly bored when the intricacies of the characters' lives are discussed in mind-numbing detail at the dinner table.

RARITY

9 – Judging from my loved ones and from what I observe, I can safely say that there are millions of them.

SEASONAL VARIATIONS

None, and with anything between two and four hours of soap operas being televised every day the Soap Obsessed will have their addiction continuously topped up. This means that they will be able to discuss the ins and outs of each show and its characters almost all the time.

AVOIDANCE|REVENGE STRATEGIES

1. Never watch soaps; there are many other things you can do with your life, if only you'd get off the sofa…

2. Never get home before nine o'clock at night.

3. Create a soap opera that that revolves around the Soap Obsessed. Ensure the characters are obese, have little in the way of social skills, hold down menial jobs and have no friends.

4. Smash up the television.

5. Write to your local politician and demand that the soaps are taken off the air because they corrupt the minds of the young and make middle-aged people fat.

☐ Tick here when you have spotted the Soap Obsessed

RATE THE
SOAP OBSESSED'S
ANNOYANCE

The Speed Camera

GENERAL CHARACTERISTICS

In the course of writing the three Pains books, I have yet to any include any inanimate objects. But I must make an exception on this occasion. Although the nature and diversity of the human race means there are plenty of painful people out there, the Speed Camera ranks amongst them even though it is a hunk of metal with a camera inside. The Gatso camera was invented by Maurice Gatsonides, a former Dutch rally driver, who as far as I'm concerned has a lot to answer for. The Speed Camera is designed to capture reckless motorists who don't understand the purpose of having a speed limit. Such people should, of course, be prosecuted and taken off the road; indeed, the need for safety was one of the principal reasons why they were introduced. However, it seems that more sinister things are happening. Since their introduction in 1996, the number of speed cameras has increased to something in the region of 4,500. Now that's a lot of cameras and a lot more than you'd need for just accident hotspots. In all some three million cars are photographed every year, which is around 10 per cent of motorists. Now assuming that each offender pays their fine (which is a big if), and that the fine is sixty pounds a throw, Speed Cameras bring in a whopping £180 million every year. Yet another great way for the Chancellor to get his hands on our money. A mere eight years ago they only collared 260,000 motorists, but clearly that was not enough. It won't be long before the police will be using handheld lasers to capture speeding motorists over a mile away. The camera, ProLaser III, will be used by coppers hiding in bushes and has nothing to do with raising any more revenue from the beleaguered motorist. Nothing. Not a thing. No way. Right? And to top it all, local councils are selling speed cameras to old women in villages so they can nab the evil motorists zooming through the quiet streets of the countryside. The problem

with this is that you will then need the police to protect the old women in villages from getting the excrement kicked out of them when the motorists get very, very angry. Not satisfied with having cameras for the speeding motorists there are also three equally annoying variants:

- The **Mobile Camera**. These cunning devices are transported around in white vans and usually parked up on the edge of urban areas, such as villages. Once in place, the doors are flung open and a policeman will sit there all day clocking anyone doing more than a mile over the speed limit.
- The **Bus Lane Camera**, which nabs anyone driving in a bus lane. Sure, I can see the importance of this in major cities, but there are cases where the only place you can drive is in the bus lane because there is no other route to your destination.
- The **Congestion Charge Camera**, which is designed to keep cars out of major cities. If you drive into somewhere like London you have to pay five pounds a day. If you fail to pay within 24 hours you are fined. So successful has the congestion charge been that other towns and cities around the country are getting on this money-spinning bandwagon. Unfortunately shops and businesses are going to the wall as people steer clear of urban areas.

Collectively, these bloody cameras are causing rebellion. Police officers are regularly being called money grabbers and many people are refusing to pay the fines. You can't blame them. Thankfully there are those who have started to take revenge. Some motorists have sprayed the lenses of the cameras, whilst others have set fire to them. There is even a guy who calls himself Captain Gatso who travels the country destroying, disrupting and defacing speed cameras. Captain Gatso leads a group known as Motorists Against Detection (MAD) who are hell bent on fighting for the beleaguered motorist everywhere. Captain Gatso and his band of merry men have won the support of drivers across the country. In fact he is the latter-day Robin Hood. If only there was more than one of him.

ANNOYANCE RATING

10 – Ten out of ten for the Speed Camera. Driving along and seeing that double flash in your rear view mirror is a gut-wrenching experience, as is the wait for the penalty notice and fine. With more and more of us being caught out for travelling a poxy one or two miles an hour above the speed limit, it's no wonder we are getting mightily fed up. When you think there are more serious crimes to address, it also makes us very upset.

RARITY

9 – It seems to me that Speed Cameras have been breeding like rabbits over the past few years. As soon as the police and local authorities cottoned onto the moneymaking opportunities they presented, they popped up everywhere. You can now see them on country lanes, roadworks, in towns, cities and blind bends. No matter where you go you will be faced with the Speed Camera.

SEASONAL VARIATIONS

None. If only there were.

AVOIDANCE/REVENGE STRATEGIES

1. Always stick to the speed limit.

2. Only use routes where there are no fixed speed cameras, like motorways or in the remotest parts of Scotland.

3. Enlist the help of Captain Gatso and his band of merry men.

4. Infiltrate the Gatso Company and sabotage the design of the camera so that it only works if you are travelling at the speed of light.

5. Blow up the Speed Cameras with explosives.

☐ Tick here when you have spotted the Speed Camera

RATE THE
SPEED CAMERA'S
ANNOYANCE

The Stressed-Out Shopper

According to some, we are a nation of shopkeepers. I actually think we are a nation of rampant consumers who can't get enough of being in shops. It's our national pastime, swarming into shopping centres and running up debt on our credit cards. Apparently we buy way too much stuff even to fill our houses. The latest trend for shoppers everywhere is to rent out self-storage units and fill them full of the trash we can't stop buying but can no longer store. Take shoes – apparently there are women out there who have bought so many pairs of shoes that the only place they can store them is in some out-of-town storage depot. They will pop out to their storage container each weekend to look at them. Surely it would be better to wear them? There are 40,000 of these units in the United States alone and it won't be long before the UK has 3,000. It's no wonder, then, that there are so many Stressed-Out Shoppers all desperately trying to fill their homes with stuff and inventory they will never use; it's worse than Christmas, as at least the things you get then and don't want have been bought by other people. According to one survey "retail therapy", as we euphemistically call it, is one of the most emotionally and physically taxing experiences of our lives. In fact, it is worse than being caught in a traffic jam (which you normally are as you attempt to reach the out-of-town megaplex), or having an argument with a partner (which once again you will almost certainly have whilst out shopping). Heart rate and blood pressure also increases significantly. So why on earth do we do it? The main reason is that shopping has become our principal pastime. It also has a lot to do with our compulsive need to keep up with our friends and neighbours. It they buy the latest hi-fi, you must too. If they buy a sports car, you'll feel inadequate until you possess one too. This obsession soon spirals out of control with you spending every

minute of your spare time shopping. There is also a gender dimension to the Stressed-Out Shopper. Let's face it, chaps, none of us like shopping; the crowed shopping malls, the constant shift from one store to another and the endless waiting outside dressing rooms (nearly always without anywhere to sit). But wait, apparently single men are getting in touch with their shopping gene and spending more time around shopping centres in order to pick up chicks.

One of the closest allies of the Stressed-Out Shopper is the Shopaholic. These are the people who cannot stop spending vast amounts of money in shops. Celebrities are well known for it, wasting tens of thousands of dollars on shite. But the most bizarre story involved a woman in the US who blew $20,000 on clothes and beauty products, only to find that she couldn't afford to pay for it all and was about to be made bankrupt. To avoid the inevitable she set up a website to seek financial help from anyone who'd give it, and give it they did. People responded in their thousands, she paid off her debt, has since written a book about her exploits and there is even a film being made. God knows who'd want to watch it. Thankfully, help is at hand for the Stressed-Out Shopper in the form of Retail Reverends. The Retail Reverend, although somewhat localised in the North of England, is a new phenomenon designed to reduce the stress of the poor old shopper. The Retail Reverend is there to provide you with a shoulder to cry on, spiritual advice – and to tell you where the vodka is. The idea is proving to be so successful that shops are now catering for all denominations and beliefs. They'll be having the devil in their stores next. Then there is the guy in the US who believes the best place to de-stress from shopping is the carwash. Not only can you wash your car, but you can also pick up some fantastic gifts for all the family as well. I'd like to see you explain why you bought your wife *The 50 Best Trucking Themes Ever* for Christmas.

ANNOYANCE RATING

7 –Fighting your way through obnoxious shoppers is an awful experience that cannot be matched. The pushing, shoving and generally discourteous behaviour is enough to drive you to drink. On the average shopping trip you will be knocked into by these toerags up to twice every minute. It should come as no surprise that the majority of people experience an increase in violent thoughts towards their fellow spendthrifts when out shopping.

RARITY

5 – As the advertisers continue to weave their seductive magic we will all find ourselves pulled into the black hole of obsessive shopping behaviour. With work consuming most of our waking hours, we feel increasingly obliged to rush out in what little time we have to spare and spend like crazy. The Stressed-Out Shopper, it seems, is here to stay.

SEASONAL VARIATIONS

You will certainly see much more of the Stressed-Out Shopper around Christmas and especially on **Christmas** Eve when all the men, who have left it too late, rush out to buy last minute gifts for their loved ones. The **January sales** are also a time to spot the Stressed-Out Shopper. At both times they have this awful tendency to get violent. The thought of watching grown adults

fighting over the latest-craze toy, such as Buzz Lightyear or Teenage Mutant Ninja Turtles, brings tears to my eyes even now.

AVOIDANCE|REVENGE STRATEGIES

1. Avoid shopping at all costs. Buy everything over the internet.

2. Use a personal shopper.

3. Hire some bodyguards to make sure no one bumps into you.

4. Seek professional help from your GP by asking them to check you into the Priory for post-shopping stress disorder.

5. When out shopping start running around whilst laughing uncontrollably. Not only will this give you more space as the other shoppers give you a wide berth, but it will also allow you to get to the front of the queue.

☐ Tick here when you have spotted the Stressed-Out Shopper

RATE THE
STRESSED-OUT SHOPPER'S
ANNOYANCE

The Supermarket Sadist

Convenience, value for money, choice, customer service: it's all there in your local supermarket. The days of having to traipse from one specialist shop to another to complete your week's shopping or pop into town every morning have long since gone. Supermarkets are everywhere and part of our everyday life. Sure, it's great to be able to pick up everything you need from one shop, but it's hardly fun, is it? What makes it such a terrible experience? Yes, you've guessed it, your fellow human beings. Attempting to complete your shopping whilst being attacked by errant trolleys, unruly kids, old women who push and shove as well as the Dawdlers, Queue Jumpers, gossipers and shelf stackers is more akin to running the gauntlet in a Roman amphitheatre than a relaxing jaunt around a shop. The people you meet, but would rather not, are known as the Supermarket Sadists. The particular subspecies to watch out for are:

- The **Trolley Twits**, who will use their trolleys as battering rams, barging their way past you on the way to their destination. As far as they are concerned you are legitimate collateral damage. They will claim that the trolley is out of control, but how can they explain the razor wire wrapped around it? The Double Trolley Twit is even worse. These are the people who decide it's time to shop for an entire year and leave a trail of destruction in their wake as they attempt to push two trolleys around unaided.
- The **Aisle Blockers**, who will decide to fill an aisle with their overweight frames and trolleys whilst chatting to their many friends. They will be at it for hours, moving from one acquaintance to the next. Why can't they go to a café like any sane person? I don't know. Maybe the supermarket is the only place where they can have social intercourse.

You will notice that most of the Aisle Blockers are pensioners with time to waste; if I see anyone I know in the supermarket, I avoid them like the plague.

- The **Screaming Brats**, who will roll about on the floor yelling and crying because their mothers aren't going to buy them their favourite cereal. The mother and the many onlookers watch in collective embarrassment, with the latter thinking to themselves, you guessed it, "crap parent". Sometimes you see the mother walk off or even pick the tyke up by the hair.
- The **Thieving Bastards,** who will walk around the shop eating various products like crisps, chocolates and biscuits, feeding said items to their screaming brats and then omitting to pay for them at the till. Who said there is no such thing as a free meal?

The saddest thing, when it comes to supermarkets, is singles night. So there you are, a single young man or woman who is desperate to get hooked up or, let's be frank about it, have a shag. What to do? Do you go down the disco to pick up some of the local talent? No. Do you ring your local lonely hearts club? No. Do you get in contact with one of your exes? No. You go to the supermarket, of course, what a fantastic idea! Whoever indulges in such behaviour really doesn't deserve to breathe. Getting hot and steamy over a fillet of halibut isn't what dating is about, is it? I guess at least you can talk about the ridiculous situation you find yourself in and you might even be able to fit in a quickie next to the frozen pizzas.

The other thing I have observed with the Supermarket Sadists is their predilection to shop on a Saturday. Now, I don't really understand this because many supermarkets are open 24 hours a day (if you are a hungry insomniac you can still get your weekly shop in) and Saturdays are possibly the worst day to shop. The supermarket is heaving; people are smashing into each other and wasting what little free time they have battling it out with the Trolley Twits. How about being smart and going during the week? Mind you, Saturdays are nowhere near as bad as any day in the run up to Christmas, Easter – or any other Bank Holiday, come to that. At this time it would be difficult to place a fag paper between the hoards of shoppers desperate to get their produce, even though the shop will be open again in a couple of days. It's as though they can't survive without the additional 10 bottles of whisky or 30 packets of bog roll.

ANNOYANCE RATING

7 – Few people actually enjoy the experience of shopping in a supermarket despite what all the adverts will tell you. The large chains would have us believe that shopping in their stores is a wholesome, rewarding experience. What toss, it's possibly the worst way to spend an hour or two. Having your shins cracked open, trying to avoid the grannies with their oversized handbags and watching filthy urchins shoving chocolate into their charming faces is enough to make you want to return to the idyllic world of the eighteenth century.

RARITY

10 – With specialist shops closing down as fast as supermarkets are expanding, the number of Supermarket Sadists will continue to grow. Soon the only place we will be able to buy anything will be from one of the major chains.

SEASONAL VARIATIONS

The Supermarket Sadist is, of course, with us **all year round** – especially on Saturdays – but there will be times when they will come out in force. You will see many more of them at Christmas, Easter, and any Bank Holiday weekend. You will also see them when there is a health scare, threat of nuclear war, ice age or sunny weather (when they will descend on the supermarket to get their barbecue fluid and briquettes). Such people are the Panic Buyers of the world who are stupid enough to believe that everything is going to run out. Though in the case of nuclear war I suppose they wouldn't be around long enough to enjoy their purchases.

AVOIDANCE/REVENGE STRATEGIES

1. Start a "keep shopping special" campaign by emphasising the benefits of shopping at your local traditional stores.

2. Always shop in the early hours of the morning. The shop may be full of perverts, but at least it's quiet.

3. Hacksaw the wheels off the Supermarket Sadist's trolley.

4. Open your own supermarket chain that will only allow certain elements of society to shop at certain times. For instance, pensioners on a Tuesday morning; parents with children after midnight and stressed-out business people between 5.00 p.m. and 6.00 p.m. on a Friday (just to ensure their stress levels remain high).

5. Tie fifteen trolleys together and see how long it takes you to create gridlock.

☐ Tick here when you have spotted the Supermarket Sadist

RATE THE
**SUPERMARKET
SADIST'S**
ANNOYANCE

The Surly Shop Assistant

GENERAL CHARACTERISTICS

One of the first jobs I had was working as a shop assistant in a department store. I had to stand up all day long being nice to pompous middle-aged men who would take forever to make up their minds and who generally treated me with contempt. I can conclude from my decades of working experience that being a shop assistant has to be one of the worst jobs you can possibly do, so it's no wonder that there are so many Surly Shop Assistants. The Surly Shop Assistant is there to top off a bad shopping experience. You may have survived the Dreadful Drivers to get to the shop in the first place. You may have also navigated a safe route through the Raging Bulls fighting it out for the remaining car parking spaces and you may have even coped with all the Stressed-Out Shoppers barging into each other and battling over the merchandise. Then you get to the point where you can pay. This should be the easiest part of the process. Well, perhaps not. One poor guy was hoping to purchase some decorative bags for a gift he had purchased. Luckily he spotted some on offer, three for the price of two. He took three to the checkout. When he reached the till the checkout assistant demanded more than the amount he was expecting to pay; he reminded the woman that they were on special offer, but to no avail. She pointed out to him that there were no offer labels on the bags so he would have to pay full price. After a few minutes of debate the manager was called and the discussions continued. As there were no labels it was decided that the bags were not on special offer. The manager disappeared and the poor consumer decided to purchase just the one, which was in any case, all he needed. Unfortunately, this required the manager's intervention again because the original amount had already been rung up. There was now an enormous queue of angry shoppers extending right to the back of the

store. When the manager arrived he was beaming from ear to ear, saying that the goods were indeed discounted and that the till would have automatically calculated the discount. After some further investigation, it transpired that the woman on the till had rung up four items instead of three, hence the mistake. This story highlights a number of observations we can make about the Surly Shop Assistant. One, they have no brains left and are therefore incapable of solving a problem without a manager's intervention. Two, they take little care over their job, but then as it entails moving a barcode over a reader and taking money from people you can see how difficult it might be to maintain concentration. Three, they would rather be anywhere in the world than serving you. Their vacant expression says it all. Finally, of course, they believe the customer is always wrong.

There are a few types of assistant you might see from time to time. The first is the one that believes you are not suitable for their store. This typically occurs in exclusive shops that sell overpriced goods. These assistants pass by you with their noses firmly stuck in the air and give you that look that suggests that you can't afford anything. The next one you'll come up against is Mr Braincell. Mr Braincell (who can be male or female but is ever and always Mr Braincell) has only one brain cell and is incapable of providing you with the information you require. When asked about whether they have a pair of shoes you love in a different size they will look at you with a blank expression and say "Dunno". Even when asked if they could check, they hover around the storeroom and come back with "Nah, nuffink in stock". Of course they haven't checked. It seems that the average shop assistant's knowledge of the products they stock is verging on the subnormal. The final variety, and one that is especially annoying, is the assistant who ignores you. You can be standing at the till for hours whilst they busy themselves doing everything they can to avoid serving you. Many will look as though they are deeply engrossed in some kind of stocktaking exercise, others will be talking to their fellow assistants who are not serving anyone either and a few will be on the telephone, again doing all they can to steer clear of what they are paid to do. And they like to call shopping "retail therapy".

ANNOYANCE RATING

7 – It's the way the Surly Shop Assistants ignore you that grates the most. They stand there looking as though they are miles away or talking to their prepubescent friends about the parties they're going to that evening instead of paying attention to what they should be doing. Even the more diligent shop assistants find them annoying.

RARITY

8 – Let's face it, we have so many goddamn shops that we can't really avoid the Surly Shop Assistants. They are everywhere, 99 per cent of them don't want to be on the other side of the counter – and it shows. Until such time as there are robots serving us we will have little choice but to deal with them. The only alternative is to shop over the internet, but then you might never get your goods. And heaven only knows what else your credit card might be used to buy.

SEASONAL VARIATIONS

The Surly Shop Assistant's seasonal behaviour is defined by the time of day and the time of year. You will see plenty of them **towards the end of a busy day**, when they are tired out and the last thing they want to see is yet another customer. Similarly you will see loads of them during **the sales season**, which is possibly the worst time to shop, let alone deal with the poor attitude of the staff.

AVOIDANCE/REVENGE STRATEGIES

1. Turn your back on shopping forever and live as a subsistence farmer.

2. Complete your transaction as quickly as you possibly can in order to minimise your contact with the Surly Shop Assistants.

3. Offer them an intensive course on customer care.

4. Spend hours in the shop getting them to fetch items from the storeroom. Then, at the end of it, tell them that you prefer the service you get from the store next door.

5. Go up to them and say, "Cut the attitude, you're just a shop assistant".

☐ Tick here when you have spotted the Surly Shop Assistant

RATE THE
SURLY SHOP ASSISTANT'S ANNOYANCE

The Swimming Pool Prat

GENERAL CHARACTERISTICS

Swimming is very good for you. Adults and children alike love going swimming, whether it's in the sea, in rivers or in leisure centres. Swimming pools are very different from what they used to be; when I was a kid, all we had was an oblong pool with perhaps the odd diving board. Today we have rapids, flumes, tubes, lazy rivers and weird shapes that you could never hope to actually swim in. These changes in design have attracted a greater number of us to the swimming pool than ever before. In summer they will be packed with people from every walk of life which means that you will, without a doubt, bump into the Swimming Pool Prat. The Swimming Pool Prat is someone who annoys you and your fellow pool users with their behaviour. The principal ones are:

* The **Keep Fit Fatties.** You have to admire the Keep Fit Fatties for their desire to shed a few hundred pounds. But they do look somewhat comical as they practice their "aquarobics" in the baby pool or shallow end. They stand in lines listening intently to the instructor as they hold onto colourful bendy foam tubes. They will move their overweight frames in unison to the instructions and sway their tubes from left to right. They look like beached whales and I can't see how standing in a swimming pool with a tube is really going to help them lose as much weight as they might do if they actually did some swimming.
* The **Lane Luvvies** who turn up day after day, after day, after day to swim in the slow, semi-fast or fast lane. They diligently swim their allotted thirty or fifty circuits looking serious and barely cracking a smile; well, swimming in lanes is utterly boring. These are the sort of people who make matchstick models and collect stamps.

* The **Lazy River Lovers**. The lazy river is fantastic fun. You don't have to expend much effort to whizz round the circuit quite fast. With the water propelling you, you are free to do what you like and some people take this to the extreme. The Lazy River Lovers are people who take the opportunity to have sex as they go round. Now I am not saying this is easy because I have never tried it, but some pool users are clearly nimble enough to succeed. One chap was in the pool with his children one Sunday evening when he came across a young couple, probably in no more than their late teens. The guy was Chav-like, in that he had the ubiquitous gold chain slung round his neck, and the girl was spotty with buck teeth. They were petting heavily when they entered the lazy river, but it was only when the chap was swimming underwater that he noticed the couple's embrace had changed. The girl had her bikini bottoms drawn to the side and the lad had his trunks pulled down to his thighs. This change of dress was accompanied by a furious moving of the lad's hips as he was desperately trying to climax whilst maintaining his balance. It was hardly an entertaining sight. Needless to say the guy witnessing the spectacle decided it was time to get out of the pool and go home.
* The **Baby Bowel Movers**. I used to take my children to the baby pool when they were very young. It was the ideal place to get them used to the water and begin the process by which they could learn to swim. Being young, many of the newcomers were unable to control themselves, which was very unfortunate. Every now and then you would have to evacuate the pool as a stream of urine or the contents of sweet Fiona's bowels were emptied into the pool. The panic on peoples' faces was rapidly followed by a stampede, with parents and children fleeing in horror as fragments of excrement drifted towards them. It was like a scene from Jaws.

In addition to the indoor pools that we all go to, there are also those that are outside. On holiday the poolside is, as we saw earlier, a hotly contested area, particularly between the Brit Abroad and the German tourist. It is also where you will see plenty of slobs seeing if they can contract skin cancer in one sitting.

ANNOYANCE RATING

5 – As long as the pool is quite empty you can tolerate the Swimming Pool Prats, but when it is busy they are very annoying. Being thrown together with a load of semi-naked people is not much fun, especially when they constantly barge into you. The other thing that irritates fellow swimmers are those users who decide to bring up as much phlegm as they can and spit it into the pool. I sometimes wonder what I am swimming through.

RARITY

8 – We humans have a special relationship with water because we are around 60 per cent water ourselves. This explains why we love spending time near or in any source of water, so long as it is not overrun with sewage. Of course, those who can't swim, which tend to be the older generation, don't like the pool, but you may still see them hanging around the shallow end instead.

SEASONAL VARIATIONS

Swimming pools are undoubtedly a **summer** thing. Everyone loves to splash around in the sun and cool off. This is especially the case with outside pools. The serious swimmers will frequent indoor pools because they are dull enough and they like to avoid having any fun at all. However, a lot of people do come to the pool in **winter**, especially those who need a wash.

AVOIDANCE/REVENGE STRATEGIES

1. Stay on dry land.

2. Build a private pool in your garden and don't let anyone but yourself use it.

3. Add chemicals to the pool which react with bodily fluids. This will act as an early warning system for the Swimming Pool Prat's emissions, from whatever orifice.

4. Empty your bowels in the pool and time how long it takes everyone to escape.

5. Find the plug and pull it out.

☐ Tick here when you have spotted the Swimming Pool Prat

RATE THE
SWIMMING POOL PRAT'S
ANNOYANCE

The Tardy Tradesman

GENERAL CHARACTERISTICS

You have taken a day off work to wait for a plumber to turn up and fix your central heating system. When you made the appointment, you were told that he would turn up at nine o'clock sharp. It's now half past three in the afternoon and he is nowhere to be seen. You ring up, complain and then repeat the whole exercise at least three more times until a) someone finally turns up, b) you go elsewhere or c) you decide to wear more layers of clothing. When they do arrive, you have to suffer the rolling of the eyes, the shaking of the head and the sharp intake of breath as you describe the nature of your predicament. Once you have completed your description they will explain to you in immense detail why the problem is more severe than they first thought. You have been ransomed to the point where you feel obliged to say "yes" to whatever their outrageous demands are in the belief that they will be able to make the problem go away. The Tardy Tradesman is the bane of our lives. Not just content with turning up late, they will also:

- Charge you huge amounts of money for what appear to be very straightforward jobs. The way they do this is to charge you a call-out fee, which covers you for their first hour of their time and, once they have spent a second over that initial hour, will charge you an extortionate hourly rate on top. I have heard of plumbers coming in to tighten up leaking radiators and invoicing the poor homeowner with £50. Worse still is when they come out, make an assessment which requires no work and still charge the call-out fee.
- Fool you into thinking the problem they are attempting to fix is more complex and costly than you could have ever imagined. They will add additional and superfluous activities and requirements to their work to ensure they can get even more cash from you. One particular Tardy Tradesman charged pensioners up to £5,000 to complete minor repairs that would have cost less than £100. Fortunately he is now making repairs of a different kind behind bars.

- Make an appalling job of fixing the problem, either leaving you with a greater problem than the one you started with, or just walk away not giving a toss. I heard of one chap whose house was rented out whilst he was overseas. A plumber was called in to fix a leak and in order to access the offending pipe pulled the ceiling down. Having made good the fix, he left leaving the owners with a rather nice if unintentional mezzanine floor. When challenged, he claimed that the ceiling had collapsed due to the damage caused by the leaking pipe. On closer inspection, you could see the marks left by his saw and it took months to sort this out with the insurance company.
- Leave a job half complete either claiming to be missing a part, or stating that they have another job on. All this means is that the problem you wanted fixing will take even longer to resolve. Sometimes they never come back. Clearly some Tardy Tradesmen have Alzheimer's.
- Do work which they are not qualified to undertake. There are probably thousands of rogue tradesmen who roam the streets offering to fix your plumbing, central heating and electrical problems for which they are clearly not qualified. The fact that you might die as a result of their incompetence is really neither here nor there.

There is a chronic shortage of good tradesmen. As everyone has rushed into white-collar jobs the number of people pursuing jobs that involve getting their hands dirty has slowed dramatically. Up until recently everyone wanted to be an investment banker or consultant and no one wanted to wear blue overalls and put their hands down blocked U-bends. All this has changed because of the dawning realisation that there are just not enough tradesmen to go round. Supply is low and demand is high. As a result, having a trade has become the hottest career around and people are leaving their high-flying city jobs to become electricians and plumbers. They claim to be leaving for lifestyle reasons but it's really because they can make a cool £70,000 fixing pipes, rewiring houses and ripping off unsuspecting customers.

ANNOYANCE RATING

8 – The Tardy Tradesmen rate pretty high in terms of annoyance. The principal reasons for this have been summarised above, but the key ones are their terrible timekeeping and the way they rip people off in order to make a fast buck.

RARITY

7 – Because there are so few tradesmen around these days, the opportunity to set yourself up as a plumber, electrician, heating engineer or any other trade, come to that, is all too easy. Without regulation, any Tom, Dick or Harry can and make plenty of cash preying on helpless pensioners and incompetent Do It Yourselfers. Many do.

SEASONAL VARIATIONS

You will see many more Tardy Tradesmen during the **winter** months when we have to deal with all kinds of domestic emergencies including leaking roofs, burst pipes, flooding, power failures, broken down central heating systems and gas leaks. Whatever the problem you can guarantee the Tardy Tradesman will be right round... well, maybe in a week or two.

AVOIDANCE|REVENGE STRATEGIES

1. Learn to fix everything yourself.

2. Always check out the qualifications and expertise of any tradesman who crosses your threshold.

3. Buy a blue boiler suit, material tool bag, some wrenches and boiler parts and smear grease on your face. Before you know it, you'll have a client list as long as your arm.

4. On completion of the job, issue the Tardy Tradesman with an invoice for all the time you have wasted waiting.

5. Video all their work and send it into the television show Rogue Traders.

☐ Tick here when you have spotted the Tardy Tradesman

RATE THE
TARDY TRADESMAN'S
ANNOYANCE

The Tourist

ourism is the lifeblood of many of the world's economies. These days there are so many different types of tourism available that you would be hard-pressed not to find something to cater to your particular tastes. From eco-tourism, where you can pollute even the remotest parts of the planet, to sex tourism, where you can pop down to Southeast Asia to get your rocks off, you name it, someone out there will sell you a trip to it, even if it happens to be a war zone – and yes, there are tourists who want to travel to places like Afghanistan. If you're anything like me when you're overseas, you will fumble around looking out of place whilst desperately trying to look cool and in control. The reality is that the locals will look at you in that knowing way that tells you that they think you're a bit of a jerk. It's one thing being overseas, where it is perfectly acceptable for you to look and behave like a fish out of water, but woe betide any overseas visitor doing it here. Welcome to the Tourist. The Tourist shares many of our characteristics when overseas, not least our ability to look completely out of place. They will wander around the streets looking dazed, confused and usually overburdened by gifts from those terribly tacky shops: you know, the ones that sell policeman's helmets, mugs with the Queen's face on and T-shirts that say "My parents went to England and the only thing they bought me was this lousy T-shirt". People are clearly stupid if they buy such shite. There are two particular types of tourist that annoy the pain spotter more than any other. These are:

* The **Small-Minded Moron**, who believes the country is the size of a postage stamp. These people will come up to you and ask if you know so and so, who lives in Glasgow, Scotland. They will also ask if you can drive from London to Scotland in an hour. What is

it with these people, have they never seen a map?

- The **Crazy Cameraman** who insists on capturing an overseas experience by photographing and videoing everything in sight. They'll photograph their friends standing next to red telephone boxes, on the Tube, beside major monuments, sitting on top of a tramp and beside anything that could be considered quintessentially British. The other thing they do is to ask you to take photos of them and their friends, or block thoroughfares as they attempt to get that perfect snap. They will also video everything in sight. When the Crazy Cameramen get back home, they typically subject their friends and neighbours to tedious video shows of all the crap places they have visited. Thankfully, copious amounts of alcohol, illegal drugs and the odd razorblade or two allow their friends to get through the experience almost sane.

One of the funniest stories I heard involved a guy (yet to be identified) creating a bogus dictionary for Japanese tourists travelling to the US. This dictionary, which sold in the tens of thousands, provided the tourists with the wrong phrases. So instead of asking "May I have a film for my camera?" they would actually say "Would you place your copious breasts in my mouth?" Another example involved a man asking "I am lost, which way is uptown?" which in fact translated to "I know martial arts. May I kick your ass?". Of course, the consequences have not been especially pleasant; tourists have been beaten up, locked up and chased down the street. Although it is hard for the Japanese involved to see the funny side, I do. The other thing I have noticed about Tourists is that many are grossly overweight. Now, one could argue that it is only the overweight wealthy businessman and his family who can afford to holiday in far-flung places. Students don't count, because they tend to sleep rough, eat food out of dustbins and generally travel with huge rucksacks on their backs.

ANNOYANCE RATING

8 – In the main, we should be grateful that the Tourists want to visit our sceptred isle; after all it adds to the general economy and hopefully reduces the amount of taxes we have to pay (some hope). I would rather they paid than us, wouldn't you? The problem is that the Tourists are very annoying because of the way they ask stupid questions, assume you know everyone in the whole of the country and litter the street with their photographic equipment. They are also notorious Queue Jumpers, as we saw in a previous entry.

RARITY

6 – The number of Tourists is increasing. With the advent of cheap flights the number of Tourists everywhere has increased dramatically. Despite the occasional recession, the rise and rise of the Tourist continues. However, once the oil runs out, we can kiss goodbye to them all and return to a pastoral existence.

SEASONAL VARIATIONS

As you would expect, the Tourists come out en masse during the **summer** months when it is beautiful. Only the diehards turn out in the wet and windy winter weather.

AVOIDANCE|REVENGE STRATEGIES

1. Avoid any tourist attraction during the summer months.

2. Whenever asked for directions send the Tourists off in the wrong direction. Better still, send them to a strip joint.

3. When asked to take their pictures, pop the camera down your trousers and give them something more interesting to show their friends.

4. Set up a stall selling tacky gifts.

5. Creep up behind them and cut off their camera straps.

☐ Tick here when you have spotted the Tourist

RATE THE
TOURIST'S
ANNOYANCE

The Toxic Teenager

GENERAL CHARACTERISTICS

Being a teenager is a tricky affair. On the one hand you are no longer a child and hate being referred to as "sonny" or being offered the child menu in restaurants, whilst on the other you are not an adult, so are not eligible to do all the things that adults do, like have sex, vote, get drunk and so on. Mind you, judging from the behaviour of the Toxic Teenager, you'd think they were adults. The Toxic Teenager is the product of the type of middle-class Crap Parent who has listened to all the pop psychology coming from crackpot child experts. Such people love to explain away the teenager's appalling behaviour using psychological bullshit which somehow exonerates the parents' lack of discipline. So if your teenager is diagnosed with attention deficit hyperactivity all it means is that they can't bothered to knuckle down and pay attention at school. Still, if you can pump them full of Ritalin to calm them down, who cares? We must not forget the Toxic Teenagers created by the lower and upper classes. The former will tend to sell drugs, mug people and steal cars, whilst the latter will take drugs, be mugged and have their lovely sports cars that daddy bought them stolen. Toxic Teenagers demand constant attention from all around them, whether it is at home, at school or around town. They are characterised by their:

* Bad taste in clothes, which will be anti-fashion and grunge-like. You can imagine them going into a store and asking for clothes which are fifteen sizes too big. They also tend to wear T-shirts with captions like "I'm busy, you're ugly, have a nice day" or "Porn Star" because they think these make them seem rebellious. Unfortunately if they happen to be travelling with grandma, such seditious displays tend to lose their potency.

- Contempt for their parents whom they will shout at and abuse at every opportunity. The parents, being weak and pathetic, attempt to laugh it off – all their kid needs is a damn good slap.
- Desire to paint their rooms black, play obscure heavy rock and have huge lumps of metal surgically inserted into their faces.
- Apparent coolness around their mates, which normally means trying to buck the system by bunking off school, getting drunk and taking drugs.
- Lack of communication skills. Their favourite method is the grunt or hand gesture.
- Ability to do the very opposite of what others want them to do.
- Need to hang around in groups looking hard and menacing. You will spot them in shopping malls, bowling alleys, back alleys and parks. They hang around in the same way that nuclear fallout does.

Other variants of the Toxic Teenager include the Tweenager, who is just a little bit too old to be called a child and a little bit too young to be called a teenager. Tweenagers want to be adults even before they have passed through those topsy-turvy years as an adolescent. They will put on make-up and demand the latest designer clothes. As you'd expect, the advertisers have cottoned on to (and perhaps even invented) this segment of society. They will promote all manner of Tweenager products that the lovely little things pester their parents for and, invariably, get. And, at the other end of the scale, you end up with the Kippers (kids in parents' pockets eroding retirement savings) who will never leave the family home. Kippers have got it sussed. They will avoid taking on a mortgage, getting a proper job or even renting a house, even though they can often afford to. Instead they will live rent free in their parents' home, eat their food and laze around... not much change from when they were teenagers, really. Of course, it is the parents who are to blame and some would rather have their kids at home for ever, which if you ask me is a bit perverse. In my mind, those who stay at home, especially the single men, are not right in the head. Try telling your hot date that you still live at home with your mum – an instant red card.

ANNOYANCE RATING

6 – Until the Toxic Teenagers break out of those difficult teenage years they will annoy everyone they can, from old people, who will complain about their behaviour, to their parents, who moan that they can't do anything about them (when it's often their fault they are the way they are).

RARITY

7 – Teenagers are on the decrease. Before long this group in society will be outnumbered by the old age pensioners. Perhaps in a couple of hundred years they will be a precious commodity, revered and looked up to. Now that would be something.

SEASONAL VARIATIONS

You will no doubt see many more Toxic Teenagers during the **summer** when they come out from hibernation. In winter they will be firmly ensconced in their bedrooms with the obligatory "do not disturb" sign stuck to the door.

AVOIDANCE/REVENGE STRATEGIES

1. Never have children.

2. Leave your Toxic Teenagers with one of your relatives, disappear for six years and then return when they have finally turned into half-decent adults.

3. Take up meditation and seek help from an hypnotist so that you can de-stress yourself.

4. Dress up as a teenager, get your ears pierced and generally act like a jerk. Before long the Toxic Teenagers will be wearing suits, speaking properly and working on their revision timetables.

5. Set up a gang of Pensioners and take on the Toxic Teenagers at their own game; hang around shopping malls and bowling alleys looking menacing.

☐ Tick here when you have spotted the Toxic Teenager

RATE THE
TOXIC TEENAGER'S
ANNOYANCE

The Traveller

GENERAL CHARACTERISTICS

This entry is not about travelling abroad or indeed about visitors from overseas but the people we see in and around our country. These are our home-grown travellers who ruin our countryside and drive us bananas. These people are known as the Travellers, and there are three particularly virulent types:

- The **Caravan Cranks**, who clog up the roads during the summer as they pull their mobile homes from one part of the country to another. They jack-knife on the motorway, block country lanes whilst travelling at five miles per hour and prevent you from overtaking because they take up so much bloody room, especially those who seem to be pulling something that resembles an articulated lorry. Surely the prospect of being cooped up in some fibreglass box with your pucker-faced granny on a wet April weekend should leave most people cold, but not the Caravan Crank; they are obsessed with taking the portable coffin out at every opportunity. Rain or shine, they'll be out and about. The other thing that Caravan Cranks do is ruin the ambience of their neighbourhoods by leaving their caravans parked on their drives. This not only looks awful as they block out the light, but it also looks as though a Pikey (see below) is visiting. When the owner gets truly bored with the prospect of living out of a caravan they just let it disintegrate in their front garden.
- The **Pikies** who have made a life decision to live outside mainstream society. These people have decided that a life on the open road is what suits them and, of course, their pockets as they can avoid paying tax and the many fixed costs that every home owner incurs. The Pikey has a preference for setting up home in lay-bys, farmer's fields, recreation grounds or on wasteland. Once ensconced in their temporary home, they will

litter the locale with the detritus of their "natural" way of life... old cars, excrement, junk and anything else that they can't be bothered to dispose of properly. They will also pop round to your house and offer to resurface your drive with some stolen tarmac. I heard of one story that involved some Toxic Teenagers and a Pikey. The kids, as per usual, were bunking off from their sport period and driving around the countryside. After a while, they saw a lone caravan perched on the side of the road and as they passed it, they leant out of the windows and shouted a stream of obscenities (as you do). Windows up, they continued along their journey congratulating themselves on their amusing diversion. Then all of a sudden a white van appeared in the rear-view mirror. The driver turned to his mates behind him and said, "There's a van travelling very fast behind us, I think I'll pull over." "Er, no, I don't think that would be a good idea," said one of the now worried passengers, "I think it's the bloke from the caravan." The driver chose to ignore this brilliant piece of advice – a bad mistake. The white van screeched to a halt and this guy got out looking mighty fed up. Now, to describe this gentlemen as an outside toilet was doing him an injustice. He was solid and cube-like, with muscles on muscles, and looked as though he could pick up the car, contents and all, and toss it into the ditch. He forced himself through the window of the car and hurled abuse at the two guys in the front, threatening to kill them, their families and everyone who knew them. The profanities that came out from his mouth would have upset the devil himself. His parting gesture was to inform the young men that if he ever saw them again he would run them off the road. Quite right too.

- The **Hitchhikers**, who do not like to pay for travel and prefer to catch lifts from passers-by rather than take the train or bus. Popular in the swinging sixties when drivers would pick up nubile young ladies for a bit of sex as payment in kind, hitchhiking remains the preserve of the young in society. The problem with many hitchhikers is that they fail to indicate where their final destination is, which usually means that most drivers pass them by. They expect motorists to read their minds as they stand on the edge of the road looking down-at-heel with a thumb stuck out. Unless they have a sign saying "Land's End" or something similar, who knows where they are going?

ANNOYANCE RATING
4 – In the main, the Traveller is not overly annoying. However, if you happen to be a farmer then you might have other opinions, especially when you have a load of Pikies on your newly planted field of winter wheat.

RARITY
3 – There are quite a few Pikies around, but this is still a tiny proportion of the total population. Hitchhiking has lost much of its appeal because most students have cars these days, plus there are just too many perverts about. Caravan Cranks are thankfully also becoming rarer as many people have realised that owning a caravan is the fast route to social suicide.

SEASONAL VARIATIONS
There is no doubt that you will see many Travellers during the **summer** months. In particular, you will still see far too many Caravan Cranks crawling along the back lanes of Britain in the hope of finding somewhere secluded to pitch up for the night. The end of the university term will bring out more Hitchhikers when the poorest students will be trying to get home as cheaply as possible. Interestingly, you are more likely to spot the Pikies in the winter than summer, when the limited foliage on the trees and bushes provide us with a clear view of their habitat.

AVOIDANCE/REVENGE STRATEGIES
1. Never travel during the summer.

2. If you see a Hitchhiker, stop as though you are going to give them a lift. When they get near your car drive off at high speed.

3. Get a change to the planning laws to prevent people from leaving caravans anywhere near their homes.

4. Write a guidebook to the best Pikey sites in the UK. Why not get some advertising from caravan suppliers?

5. Buy a steam engine and spend your weekends blocking up the roads.

☐ Tick here when you have spotted the Traveller

RATE THE
TRAVELLER'S
ANNOYANCE

The Unexpected Visitor

ou're at home watching the television and the doorbell rings. What do you do? It's a crucial moment in your favourite soap opera and you can't bear to miss it. In the end, you decide to rush to the door in the hope that you can get rid of whoever it is quickly. You should be so lucky. You have just opened your door to the Unexpected Visitor. This pain is characterised by an annoying habit of turning up unannounced and at the most inopportune times. Unfortunately they are on a mission and won't be deterred by your pathetic attempts at getting rid of them. The types of unexpected visitor you should expect to see include:

- The **Jehovah's Witness,** who will hover at your front door in order to tell you about Jesuuuuusss. If you are smart, you can usually spot them from the other end of the street. They will be well dressed, wandering along in groups and will sport cheap-looking attaché cases in which they hold the magazines they try to thrust into your hands. The best response I find is, "I love giving blood and can't wait for my presents at Christmas."
- The **Scumbag Squatter**, who will take over your house when you are out and, with the law on their side, will trash the place and leave you with an enormous repair bill. One bunch of squatters, who had been in the same house for over two decades, were given the property by a court order. Not bad, a million-pound property, now theirs to dispose of as they please.
- The **Trick or Treater,** who has adopted the pointless American tradition of dressing up as the devil, a monster from a well-known movie, or a complete jerk in order to extract your well-earned cash. Trick or Treaters will ring on your door and say in a deadbeat

voice "Trick or treat". A swift slam of the door normally gets rid of them. If that fails, give them some laxative chocolate.

- The **Crap Carol Singers**, who will trek up your street during the run up to Christmas, knock on your door and entertain you with a terrible rendition of *Once in Royal David's City* in the hope that you will part with some cash. What's worse is when you have to endure a couple of Chavs singing on your doorstep. They may be drunk, will sing out of tune, look forlorn and stick their hands out in the expectation that you will cross their palms with gold. I can assure you the only gold that will appear will be from my bladder. Still, at least it will warm the cockles of their hearts...

- The **Dusty Dork**, who will appear at your front door on a Sunday evening holding a tray full of dusters, household cleaners and a sad face. They are typically from the sink estates of the North and will say that they are unemployed hoping to augment their paltry income from state benefits (which they may well have secured fraudulently). Why would you want to buy anything from them in the first place, but more critically, why on earth would you want to buy a duster when you already have a drawer full? It's another swift "no, thank you" and a slam of the door.

- The **Credit Creep**, who will approach the low-income consumers in society in order to dupe them into taking out an extortionate loan.

- The **Bastard Bailiff**, who will break your door down in order to remove your property to repay your debts. Of course, most of these come from the Credit Creep who duped you into taking out more debt than the gross national product of Lithuania only a few weeks earlier. Only now do you understand that they weren't charging you a standard rate of interest.

- The **Political Canvasser** who will only ever turn up on your doorstep when it's election time. They will stand there at your front door asking if they can rely on your support. The trouble is, you don't even know who they are. One chap, who wanted to get rid of a group of political grandees, said that he would support them and duly slammed the door. A month or so later they came back in an attempt to enlist the man's support. The poor guy thought he had seen the last of them. Unfortunately that was not the case and after a heated debate the group departed.

ANNOYANCE RATING

9 – The Unexpected Visitor is, put simply, irritating. If you really wanted any of these lowlifes to visit you, you would have made an appointment. But they don't understand this simple rule of engagement. They will decide when to descend on you, and its always the wrong time.

RARITY

5 – In the main, this depends on where you live. If you are lucky enough to live in a remote village, you will be spared. However, if you live on an estate, then you should expect to receive more than your fair share of Unexpected Visitors. Overall, though, we should be pleased that they are rarer than many of the public pains we are likely to spot.

SEASONAL VARIATIONS

As ever, the **summer** months will bring out more Unexpected Visitors than we would like. Winter is generally too cold and wet to attract all but the diehards; you will only spot the Jehovah's Witnesses and Dusty Dorks on such dark evenings. Others will only *(thankfully)* appear on certain days, like Halloween and Christmas week.

AVOIDANCE|REVENGE STRATEGIES

1. Move to the top floor of a block of flats.

2. Draw your curtains, turn off the lights and hide until the Unexpected Visitors have gone away.

3. Place sandbags around your house and lay mines between your front door and the pavement.

4. When they appear, why not try and sell them something instead? Better still engage them in a religious conversation which involves thrusting a magazine into *their* hands.

5. Daub a big red cross on your front door with a sign outside reading "Danger: bubonic plague". This should stop even the most persistent visitor.

☐ Tick here when you have spotted the Unexpected Visitor

RATE THE
UNEXPECTED VISITOR'S
ANNOYANCE

Afterword

So you have been nauseated by them, accosted by them and had your tranquillity disturbed by them. It seems that wherever you go you will meet someone who is only there to spoil your fun or simply make your daily life that little bit more unbearable. You may be one of the many unfortunate people in the world who has to endure Pains on a continuous basis: on the trains, in the office and in public. In other words, someone who gets no peace. It's quite amazing that any of us stay sane, but judging by the amount of people who are addicted to Prozac, I guess that must be very few. You may have also realised that you are a Pain yourself, and perhaps even a number of different ones. So how do you avoid being a Pain in public? Here are my top five ways:

1. Pain spot
2. Stay indoors
3. Join a self-help group which is designed to make you a better person
4. Live on a remote desert island
5. Become exceptionally wealthy and be the first person to live on the Moon.

And finally, please remember the Five Golden Rules for Pain Spotting. They will help you live a fulfilled, happy and enriched life.

1. NEVER JUDGE A BOOK BY ITS COVER
You mustn't be fooled by first impressions. What at first glance may seem like a commonplace Pollster might actually turn out to be a Charity Chugger who has gone AWOL. Likewise, a straightforward Unexpected Visitor may in fact be a Traveller who has lost his way. Initial appearances can count, sure, but exchanging views with a Chav might be a short cut to suicide.

2. DON'T PIGEONHOLE

Pains, like all species on the planet according to Darwin, are able to adapt, evolve, mutate and cross-fertilize. This can occasionally leave you with a chameleon-like entity to contend with. In this way, a Celeb may also be an Attention Seeker, a Protestor or a Dogger looking for the local car park. You can always tick off more than one Pain per observation. So, make your observations; do your analysis, and be sure you have got all the qualities of every Pain straight in your mind before committing yourself.

3. DON'T BE TOO JUDGMENTAL

There are two reasons for this. First, this book is about providing an amusing diversion during your daily life. Second, we are all Pains in one form or another, and as the saying goes, "People in glass houses shouldn't let their dogs crap all over the pavement".

4. DON'T GET INTO ANY FIST FIGHTS

There is no chance whatsoever that the assertion "the book told me to do it" would stand up in a court of law. Hard luck.

5. LEARN TO LOVE YOUR PAIN

This is the most testing of all the Golden Rules, but you should learn to love the Pain. For he is your brother, or maybe your Public Polluter. The Bible tells us to love our neighbours. And that means unconditionally, even the noisy ones. Even when the person in front of you is Dawdling when you are in a tearing hurry. Besides, if you don't learn to love them, you might just go mad.

So that's it, the end of the *Pains* trilogy. Collectively you have a compendium of 150 Pains that I hope you will treasure and use for years to come. Using all three books will allow you to deal with the annoying people around you in an highly effective way. And if you are one of the increasing numbers of Pain Activists you will be helping to transform society into the Garden of Eden. I hope to see you at a Pains convention very soon where we can share our stories about the painful people in the world. In the meantime watch out for my next book, *The Alternative Guide to Careers*, which will provide you with a different perspective on the types of careers we choose to follow.